GUIDE
TO LEGAL
WRITING
STYLE

GUIDE TO LEGAL WRITING STYLE

SECOND EDITION

TERRI LeCLERCQ
Senior Lecturer
University of Texas School of Law

Aspen Law and Business
A Division of Aspen Publishers, Inc.
Gaithersburg   New York

Permissions
Aspen Law & Business
1185 Avenue of the Americas
New York, NY 10036

Printed in the United States of America.

ISBN 0-7355-1225-6

1 2 3 4 5 6 7 8 9 0

Library of Congress Cataloging-in-Publication Data

LeClercq, Terri, 1946-
    Guide to legal writing style / Terri LeClercq — 2nd ed.
        p. cm.
    Includes index.
    ISBN 0-7355-1225-6
    1. Legal composition. 2. Law—United States—Language. I. Title.

KF250 .L3913 2000
808'.06634—dc21   99-058203

About Aspen Law & Business
Legal Education Division

With a dedication to preserving and strengthening the long-standing tradition of publishing excellence in legal education, Aspen Law & Business continues to provide the highest quality teaching and learning resources for today's law school community. Careful development, meticulous editing, and an unmatched responsiveness to the evolving needs of today's discerning educators combine in the creation of our outstanding casebooks, coursebooks, textbooks, and study aids.

Aspen Law & Business
A Division of Aspen Publishers, Inc.
A Wolters Kluwer Company
www.aspenpublishers.com

Dedication

This book was written to help the many legal writing faculty who have such enormous jobs: perhaps it will allow them some freedom to concentrate on analysis; on research; on effective feedback; on student progress; on developing their professional programs; on winning respect and salaries and the good-will of their faculties, administrators, and students.

I am grateful for the institutional support of the law schools at University of Texas, St. Louis University, and Catholic University of America.

Special thanks to

Mike Kolby, Director, and the Catholic Law School writing faculty;
Kay Kavanagh, Associate Dean and Legal Writing Director,
the University of Arizona;
the University of Texas writing faculty;
the St. Louis University writing faculty;
Mark Wojcik, John Marshall writing faculty;
Anne Kringel, Director, University of Pennsylvania writing faculty;
and Jack Getman, my greatest support.

SUMMARY OF CONTENTS

CONTENTS

PREFACE

So here you are in law school, and it's back to learning how to write. Why?

WHY STUDY WRITING—AGAIN?

No matter what academic and life experiences you've had, you will immediately realize that legal writing is a skill unto itself. And, like any new skill, it has to be practiced.

Yes, it's still writing, but it is a **branch** of technical writing with its own set of rules and priorities. Although you learned to write in grade school, compose essays and organize reports in high school, and perhaps created analytic discussions in college or on the job, there's more! Each of those writing stages helped you reach the next stage—and the next stage. Now you've reached a narrowed branch within the field of technical writing. It's tricky, and it's contradictory, but it reflects the very skill you learn in your law classes: getting to the essence of the matter and comparing/contrasting that essence with other cases and policies.

When you begin writing legal documents for class, you'll realize that much of legal writing is formulaic, just as much of learning to play the piano or solve mathematical problems is. Just as you have to know the scales and formulae before you can leap off into your own creations, you need to practice the basic stages of legal writing.

Legal writing is demanding in ways that undergraduate writing rarely is, perhaps because legal writing requires you to be simultaneously precise and concise. Each term in an agreement must be explicit, for instance, and yet courts' page limitations can prevent you from including those precise words in your brief.

Additionally, legal writing is driven by deadlines that carry heavy consequences: if an attorney doesn't file a motion on time, it cannot be filed later with points off the court's final "grade." Indeed, bar journals and newspapers are full of accounts of attorneys receiving sanctions—attorneys whom the court or the bar has accused of malpractice because they missed filing dates.

WHY SHOULD I CONCENTRATE ON WRITING SKILLS?
(Or, does someone really read this stuff?)

Another shock for most first-year legal writers is their new audience. In undergraduate school, it's the professor's job to read student writing. A student's job was just to turn in his or her best work (although most of us can remember turning in a "draft" as a final paper—and getting away with it). When graduates leave and start their professional roles, though, they have to fulfill the professional expectations of their audiences—just as soon as they guess who the audience is and what that new audience expects. For example, first-year engineers discover that long explanations about decisions are not acceptable to their result-oriented supervisors; and nurses quickly learn that the pace and volume of a hospital keep their shift supervisors from reading detailed summaries.

Curiously, when undergraduates enter law school, those new law students are immediately in a purgatory: they are again in an academic setting where their professors must read student writings to evaluate the underlying thinking, but the academic world also simulates the practice of law, so professors demand timely and precise/concise documents.

It's not easy to meet the new demands of law school. Professors take on the persona of typical audiences of law practice: office supervisors, court clerks, and judges. All of these real-life audiences have hectic work days filled with writing they must plow through before they can take essential action. Their clients are paying these attorneys to explain the law and give advice in nonlegal terms. Whew.

When professors add new legal terms and concepts plus the burden of multiple reading assignments, law students can crumble. Many students revert to a defensive posture and insist that they came to law school to study doctrine only—not basic writing skills. Thus they try to circumvent the very process that will help them learn doctrine, that of analyzing cases and organizing their thoughts toward a better understanding of the law. Other law students give it the old undergraduate sideswipe and hope it suffices until they have time to really concentrate on writing.

Those reactions are mistakes—costly mistakes.

Practicing legal writing is practicing the law. Learning to be concise is learning to analyze and cut extraneous arguments and words. Learning to find the precise word is learning to get to the essence of the matter. That's what law school is about, and it's how writing fits into the practice of law.

WHY IS THIS NEW AUDIENCE SO HARD TO IMPRESS?

(Or, if I sound smart enough, will I get a job?)

Visualize an audience of hurried, irritated, and probably bored readers (does this describe your first-year study group as well?). You must convince them that you have something they need to read, and that your position is correct. Your memorandum or brief or letter is not the most important part of your readers' day; it's only part of their job:

- They are not reading it uninterrupted.
- They are not reading it during mental prime time.
- They do not want to focus on your writing style.
- They are not interested in the law for law's sake.
- They do not expect to be entertained or amused.

Somehow, you have to get them to read what you've written, and to act on your ideas or conclusions. That's your job.

WHY NOT USE MY TIME FOR ALL THE IMPORTANT LAW I CAME HERE TO LEARN?

(Or, I have only 24 hours in any day and I need to read my case books, not redraft a memorandum.)

Researching and drafting an answer to a hypothetical question will train you to use case law. Organizing your answer will train you to analyze concepts, the very skill you must demonstrate on final examinations. Drafting and editing, then drafting and editing again, will prepare you for later class assignments, for final exams, and for the practice of law. Remember that part of your legal education is learning to allocate your time so you can spend that time improving your draft. In law practice, a draft is really a draft; attorneys can rework a client letter six times, or reorganize a contract fifty times!

In the practice of law, your signature will signal that you've done the best you can do. If you turn in hastily written assignments now, you will probably turn out hastily written documents when you are actually an attorney. That makes sense, doesn't it, because you will have practiced not striving for your best.

All that important law you learn from reading cases and statutes will remain theory until you test it in argument, and what better record of your thought process than the written record? First-year legal writing will help you adjust your ideas, your use of precedent, and your language. You are not taking a detour or wasting your time. You are indeed learning all that important law, in a way that you can track and defend.

IF LEGAL WRITING IS SO IMPORTANT, WHY ARE MY TEXTBOOKS FULL OF CONVOLUTED OPINIONS?

(Or, is someone kidding?)

Not many readers can defend the prose of judicial opinions selected for case books—a style students instinctively assume is "the way law looks." We can't defend this prose because it is so very terrible—you're right. Perhaps you can get some perspective if you realize that

- the case may have been written years ago when writers used a more lofty, elevated language,
- casebook authors include cases **not** for their prose style but for the issues they present, and
- there are a lot of bad writers in the legal profession—but you don't have to join them!

Historically, legal prose has been both dense and confusing. Critics of that prose (and they are, of course, legion) theorize that early writers needed both Latin and French terminology to meet the needs of a linguistically varied audience, and that the audience expected an elevated style to reflect the somber nature of the law. Some even more cynical critics insist that early legal writers wanted to make the law unobtainable to the layman so that society would always need attorneys.

Few readers today expect Latin and French equivalents, and most are depressed rather than flattered when they see a page of legal prose. Your frustration when you read your casebooks isn't what you want your own readers to duplicate; your goal is to write precisely and concisely so that readers appreciate your intelligent explanation of difficult material.

HOW CAN I MAKE BEST USE OF THIS BOOK?

1. Skim this book before beginning your first assignment; you'll see what is important to your new field.
2. After completing your first draft, check your organization against the suggestions in Chapter 1. Evaluate your sentences using the guide of Chapter 2. Make sure you haven't misused any new or unusual words by comparing yours to those in Chapter 3. Finally, review the rules of punctuation set out in Chapter 4 to ensure that you use the conventions of legal punctuation. Then you're ready to turn in your final version to the professor.

3. When your paper is returned, focus on the professor's feedback and return to any chapter that offers advice in those areas. If your reader had trouble following your analysis, perhaps you need to revise the road map or topic sentences. Carefully reread the advice of Chapter 1. Similarly, if your reader asked questions about your sentence style or word choice, review Chapters 2 and 3. You may learn that your punctuation (or lack of) created substantive questions; if so, return to Chapter 4 for help.

4. Focus on the area your professor/reader has the most concern about. Turn to the end of the book and complete the practice exercises in that area. This practice on someone else's sample sentences offers you some distance on your own problem areas. The exercises also help you realize the confusion that can result from lack of road map, convoluted sentences, misused words, or incorrect punctuation.

With this focus on improvement, you won't make the same mistakes again. You'll grow as a legal writer. Then, after repeated practice throughout law school, you can enter the legal profession unworried about an opposing counsel who is paid just to scrutinize your document for weakness in your analysis or ambiguities in your prose.

This book cannot answer all of your style questions or calm all of your anxieties. But if, as a law student, you use it as a springboard for constant and deliberate practice, you'll develop into a careful legal writer who can concentrate on your new profession.

December 1999   *Terri LeClercq*

GUIDE TO LEGAL WRITING STYLE

1

ORGANIZING WITH STYLE

After thinking about the facts of a case and tentatively labeling the problem ("this sounds like a jurisdiction problem," or "we're going to have to know whether abandoning property matters if the title is being disputed"), writers generally produce a hash of ideas, marginalia, and cases. **It's a draft**. The final product has to inform readers about the writer's ideas and the legal precedent behind those ideas.

Now, how do we get from hash to "print"? Some writers are naturally organized and begin with an outline that they fill in as the research develops. Others flail about, scribbling and drawing arrows until they understand what it is they're writing about. No matter what a writer's preliminary organizational strategy may be, readers have to be able to follow a final logical progression of ideas and to understand it. That's why as a writer, you need to reserve plenty of time beyond the original investigative researching and scribbling stage. Legal writers must tackle the draft again, with a fresh eye, and decide what their audiences should get out of the reading and how they, as writers, can best help readers find what they need. Investigating your macro and micro organization should be the first step you take.

Macro (overall) organization includes a general introduction, your decision about the order and cohesion of major points, and your conclusion. Micro (paragraph) level is your paragraph development and internal cohesion. If you give readers a strong introduction and follow it logically, readers can skim the introduction and headings and quickly know both what the document is about and how the parts fit together.

OVERVIEW

- ◆ Organize your draft—summarize each paragraph in the **margin** and cut/paste into a logical sequence.
- ◆ Decide what information the audience needs (**thesis**), move it into your introductory set-up paragraph(s), and create a **road map** anticipating your organization.
- ◆ Add **headings** that follow the language of your set-up and act as signposts.
- ◆ Introduce paragraphs with **topic sentences** that anticipate your point.
- ◆ Connect major sections and paragraphs with **transitions**.
- ◆ **Conclude** with a reminder of the set-up or offer to provide additional information.

◆ ◆ ◆ ◆

I don't care how it's organized as long as it makes
chronological or neurological sense.
Comment from a Clerk Who Was Reading a Stack of Briefs

◆ ◆ ◆ ◆

ORGANIZING YOUR RESEARCH: MARGIN OUTLINES

The hardest part of any written assignment is to evaluate what you've discovered in your research. A useful technique is to type out your ideas as you've scribbled them, putting them into whatever order seems best for the moment. That can mean typing case summaries first, or your list of policy considerations, etc. Just get them down. (Don't throw away your notes, because you'll undoubtedly need them later.) Push "print" and see what you've got.

In the margin of that draft copy, jot one word or phrase that summarizes each paragraph's main point:

facts, case 1 ▶	Mrs. Cook, nursing home employer, cannot be held accountable for discharging Mrs. Benjamin, an employee in the first stages of Alzheimer's disease.
history ▶	Ohio law, Ohio Rev. Code Ann $ 4112.01(A)(13) (Anderson 1998), requires three elements of proof. Hazlett v. Martin Chevrolet, Inc., 496 N.E.2d 478, 480 (Ohio 1986).
facts, case 2 ▶	As set out in Hazlett, the employee must prove she is handicapped as defined under Ohio statute. Id., at 480.
facts, case 3 ▶	Second, the employee must show that she was fired because of the handicap. Id.
distinguishing facts ▶	Finally, the employee must establish that she is able to "safely and substantially" perform at her job, despite this handicap. Id. Mrs. Benjamin will have dif-
leftovers ▶	ficulty establishing a prima facie case.

Then quickly read through your marginalia, checking to see if they follow a logical order. If they do, decide if that order fulfills your audience's needs. If not, you can rearrange with a massive cut-and-paste. Sometimes you'll be able to delete whole paragraphs of repetition. Occasionally you'll see a logic hole you need to plug.

INTRODUCTION: THESIS AND ROAD MAP

After you've moved your draft sections into a logical order, you need to create an introduction (which may be the first paragraph or several) that includes:

- A **thesis** announcing your major point or conclusion and
- A **road map** announcing your organization.

This internal cueing anticipates the major point(s) and divisions of organization, which allows readers to feel comfortable with what follows. A comfortable reader is a grateful reader.

The introductory paragraphs explain your main **thesis** (usually your conclusion) in the context of the overall issue. Some legal readers expect to find the conclusion attached to specific facts; other readers don't. In addition to the thesis, you will create a **road map**, which is a textual outline of the information to follow. The road map lets readers know in advance the relative *weight* of the parts and the *order* in which they will be discussed. If the overall thesis depends on several legal points, you should begin each section with a small-scale version of the introductory thesis and road map.

According to Ohio law, it is "unlawful discriminatory practice" for an employer to discriminate against a handicapped employee. In this case, Mrs. Cook, nursing home employer, cannot be held accountable for discharging Mrs. Benjamin, an employee in the first stages of Alzheimer's disease, because Mrs. Benjamin's disease keeps her from performing "safely and substantially." The plaintiff, Mrs. Benjamin, bears the initial burden of proof in a case of handicap employment and must establish a prima facie case. Ohio law, Ohio Rev. Code Ann § 4112.01(A)(13) (Anderson 1998), requires three elements of proof. Hazlett v. Martin Chevrolet, Inc., 496 N.E.2d 478, 480 (Ohio 1986). As set out in Hazlett, the employee must prove she is handicapped as defined under Ohio road map ▶ statute. Id. at 480. Second, the employee must show that she was fired because of the handicap. Id. Finally, the employee must establish that she is able to "safely and substantially" perform at her job, despite this handicap. Id. Based on the facts of this case, Mrs.

thesis ▶ Benjamin will have difficulty establishing a prima facie case and cannot meet the burden of proving that she can "safely and substantially" perform her job.

Thesis statements vary by function: the thesis of a *memorandum*, for example, is predictive, leading the reader from the legal issue to a short, general conclusion that is afterwards supported by a balanced, analytic survey of pertinent theories and cases. In contrast, the thesis of a *brief* is persuasive rather than predictive, and thus announces a conclusion that you will then support through cases and policy.

A **road map** foreshadows the organizational pattern to follow. It might be a quick overview of three exceptions to a general rule. It might be a list of theories that you will examine. Like a literal road map, it lets travelers (your readers) know how long they will be on the road, what they will find the most interesting, and which major roads will be the best along the way.

Look at the following examples from different legal documents and examine the introduction, the set-up, and the road maps for these different formats and audiences.

A brief:

thesis ▶ The Plaintiff teacher should be awarded damages for the violation of his constitutional rights because his topic was of public concern that outweighs the possibility of school disruption. Courts have recognized that "it is essential that [teachers] be able to speak out freely . . . without fear of retaliatory dismissal." Pickering v. Bd. Of Educ. Of Township High Sch., 391 U.S. 563, 572 (1968). Thus, a teacher who is terminated for the exercise of free speech will be awarded damages for the violation of constitutional rights if he proves that the statements of controversy were of public concern and were the sole cause of his dismissal. Courts will recognize only a narrow exception: if the interest of the teacher in commenting on matters of public concern is outweighed by possible disruptions that might result within the school district. See <u>Daniels v. Quinn</u>, 801 F.2d 687, 689 (4th Cir.

1 ▶ 1986). Because the Plaintiff's statements were of pub-

road map 2, 3 ▶ lic concern, addressed to a public audience, outside the

4 ▶ workplace, and unrelated to his outstanding record at the high school, this Court should find that the firing of the Plaintiff violated his Constitutional right to free speech.

A law review note:

The Security Housing Unit at Pelican Bay State Prison near Crescent City, California, is the last stop in California's penal system. It was in this unit that Vaughn Dortcha, a prisoner with a life-long history of mental problems, was confined after a conviction for grand theft. There, the stark conditions of isolation caused his mental condition to deteriorate, to the point that he "smeared himself repeatedly with feces and urine." . . . Ultimately, six guards wearing rubber gloves held Vaughn, with his hands cuffed behind his back, in a tub of scalding water. . . . After about fifteen minutes, when Vaughn was finally allowed to stand, his skin peeled off in sheets, "hanging in large clumps around his legs." . . . He went into shock and almost died. . . . Pelican Bay Warden Charles Marshall attributed the incident to an "inexperienced staff" and "the difficulties of opening a new prison."

. . .

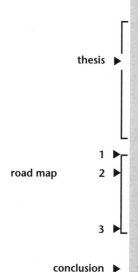

thesis ▶ This Comment argues that, rather than being a model for the rest of the nation . . . Pelican Bay State prison inflicts unacceptable psychological trauma on inmates confined in the virtually unrelieved isolation of the Security Housing and Violence Control Units . . . [and] as a result of this isolation violates the Eighth Amendment of the United States Constitution in that it constitutes cruel and unusual punishment.

road map

1 ▶
2 ▶
3 ▶

conclusion ▶

Part II provides a brief history of the American penitentiary . . . Part III describes the physical aspects of Pelican Bay and the general conditions of confinement within the Security Housing Unit (SHU) and the Violence Control Unit (VCU). Part IV demonstrates that the particular effects of sensory deprivation . . . violate the Eighth Amendment. . . . The Comment concludes with a summary of the argument and a discussion of the negative societal effects that result when psychologically damaged SHU inmates are released directly into our cities and towns.

Source: Sally Mann Romano, *If the SHU Fits: Cruel and Unusual Punishment at California's Pelican Bay State Prison*, 45 EMORY L. J., 1089–1092.

USING HEADINGS AS SIGNPOSTS

Legal writers should divide and highlight the segments of their documents with short headings and subheadings. Long documents *require* headings; shorter documents are *aided* by them. A quick glance at headings will give readers an overview of the larger picture and the picture's coherence. Headings help you as you write. Also: if the headings you add to the first draft don't summarize your discussion when you quickly skim them, or if the headings jump you from one idea to another, you can make the necessary adjustments to your draft.

Guidelines for Headings

1. Headings need to **satisfy the readers' needs.** A memorandum labeled "Element One," "Element Two," and "Element Three" does not satisfy anything. Instead, a heading should label the material within that block and summarize the analysis. The introductory paragraph below sets up logical headings that will follow:

question ▶ Our client hopes to overcome a defense motion for summary judgment. A nonmoving party is not required to prove the entire case at this stage but only genuine issues of material fact that make summary judgment inappropriate. The Supreme Court of Tennessee applied Rule 56 of the Tennessee Rules of Civil Procedure, governing summary judgments, in <u>Byrd v. Hall</u>, 847 S.W.2d 208 (Tenn. 1993). In <u>Byrd</u>, the plaintiff, a former head of hospital radiology, sued defendant physicians who had allegedly tortuously interfered with his hospital employment. To determine whether to grant the summary judgment in favor of the defendant physicians, the Court viewed the evidence in the light most favorable to the nonmoving party (plaintiff). The Court then examined (1) whether a factual dispute exists, (2) whether the disputed facts are material to the case's outcome, and (3) whether the disputed facts create a genuine issue for trial.

facts ▶

law ▶

3 prongs ▶

A. *Does a factual dispute exist*

• • •

Memorandum headings follow ▶ road map with similar language

B. *Are the disputed facts material to the case's outcome*

• • •

C. *Does the disputed fact create a genuine issue for trial*

• • •

2. Headings should **be parallel in content, grammar, and placement.** (One section may contain subheadings while other sections do not—that is perfectly acceptable.) If you insert a major heading to introduce one element of negligence and not the following two, your reader won't understand that those three elements are parallel. A bonus for careful writers is the visual effect of headings: a longer, subdivided section alerts readers that it is more complicated, or more important, to your discussion.

3. Headings can consist of single words, phrases, or sentences, but they should **be consistent in content and grammatical structure.** If the first major heading is a full sentence, then all the other major headings should be full sentences. Similarly, the subheadings may be only phrases, but then each subheading should be a phrase.

Phrase Subheadings	Sentence Subheadings
The Promise of ADA	**The Promise of ADA**
Jskfjklhdfhsdfh	*Jskfjklhdfhsdfh*
Legislative History	*Congress passed the ADA to make up for societal wrongs.*
Dfhsdhdsfkhlsdf	
The Statute	*dsf.jwloeur*
Fjaklsdfksj	*jklsd sdfkl*
EEOC Regulations	*The ADA's definition of disability is three-fold.*
hafsdhsfasdf	
sfk;oaweiufk	*hjdsfhjdsfhj*
Interpretive Guidance	*xdflisdf*
Nmdsf;p9ujklwe	*sdfowier*
	eirfldslkj
	euwrfjwauoerjou

4. Headings should be **consistent in typography**; if major subheadings are flush left and in bold face, then subsubheadings need to be differentiated as a group by a consistent indent, or they should be in italics. Several courts have specific guidelines for headings, but others do not, so you should research before assuming that one format will work for any document.

5. Headings should be **independent of the text** that follows them. The following example relies on its lengthy heading for its logic; if the readers skipped the heading, they would find themselves in the middle of a definition of proximate cause that has no context. The writer has left the context back up in the heading and has forgotten to reestablish it within the textual discussion:

> **B. According to MCLA 281.1051, an operator of a vessel has a duty to render reasonable assistance to a person affected by an accident in Michigan lakes and rivers.**
>
> However, the relationship is special for another reason, and that is the Marine Safety Act, which states:
>> the operator of a vessel involved in a collision, accident or other casualty, and the operator of any other vessel, so far as he can do without serious danger to his own vessel, crew, and passengers, shall render reasonable assistance to a person affected by the collision, accident, or other casualty. . . . [Cite.]
>
> This very broad statute essentially requires of any and all boaters and boat operators (like Surrey) a Good Samaritan duty to assist boaters in need of such aid, by any means reasonable and necessary.

TRY THESE

Skim the introductory paragraphs two students created for a similar brief topic. Are their headings, taken out of their original discussions, reasonable follow-ups to their introductions?

1. Mr. Long's statement to news reporters after a political rally was of public concern and therefore shielded as free speech. The speech's content, context, and form establish it a public concern if it touches any matter of political, social, or other community issue. <u>Connick v. Myers</u>, 461 U.S. 138, 146 (1968). The interoffice questionnaire in <u>Connick</u> did not touch on these matters primarily, and the Court held that it was not therefore of public concern. <u>Id</u>. at 148. The Court weighed heavily that the questionnaire was interoffice and addressed to matters of employment transfers within the office. Unlike <u>Connick</u>, Mr. Long's statements were of public concern in content, context, and form.

   a. The content of Mr. Long's statement advocated his political organization's platform.

•   •   •

   b. The context and form of Mr. Long's speech were a public address after a political rally in response to a reporter's questions.

•   •   •

2. To determine whether a statement is of public concern, courts weigh the content, form, and context of a given statement as revealed by the whole record. <u>Connick v. Myers</u>, 461 U.S. 138, 148 (1983). When evaluating these considerations, courts have concluded that statements are of public concern, and therefore protected by the Constitution, when they (1) are addressed to a public audience, (2) are made outside the workplace, and (3) involve content largely unrelated to the speaker's government employment. <u>United States v. Nat'l Treasury Employees Union</u>, 513 U.S. 454, 466 (1995).

   a. Mr. Long's statements were addressed to a public audience.

•   •   •

   b. Mr. Long's statements were made outside of his workplace.

•   •   •

   c. Mr. Long's statements involved content that was largely unrelated to his employment at the high school.

•   •   •

Evaluate the following heading and paragraph of section C of a brief.

c. Even if a substantial change in circumstances adversely affecting the child's welfare is proven, the District Court erred in determining that the child's best interest is served by modifying the order granting the custodial parent sole custody.

> "An order for custody of a minor child . . . shall award . . . custody of such child to such person . . . as will best promote the interest and welfare of the child." N.C. Gen. Stat. § 50-13.2. North Carolina adheres to the "best interest" test for determining child custody.

USEFULNESS OF TOPIC SENTENCES

Topic sentences work in much the same way as a thesis (see pages 4–7): they introduce the idea within the paragraph; they set boundaries for the paragraph; and they help tie ideas together. Perhaps some paragraphs won't require a specific topic sentence—they'll still need cueing transitions to help readers stay on track.

Quickly skim the following student memorandum looking **only** at each paragraph's topic sentence.[1]

MEMORANDUM

TO: Carol Richards

FROM: Heather Dean

DATE: September 21, 2000

SUBJECT: Intent element of potential battery claim against Byronita Lima by Juan Gerardi

QUESTION PRESENTED: Is the intent element of a battery claim satisfied when an actor causes unintended harm to an unintended victim?

---

[1] This sample memorandum reflects the Texas Rules of Form, a citation system Texas lawyers use to supplement the Bluebook. Under that system, decisions of the Texas Courts of Appeals are followed by a writ or petition history. Here, "writ ref'd n.r.e." means "writ [of error] refused, no reversible error."

CONCLUSION: Yes. In a battery claim, specific intent is not required with regard to the harm caused or the recipient of the harm. If an actor intended to cause particular harm to an intended victim, this intent can be transferred to an unexpected harm and to an unintended victim.

FACTS: Byronita Lima surprised two apparent thieves in the orchard of her prize-winning peach trees. When she saw the trespassers, Lima ran after them, shouting, and fired two warning shots above and to the right of them. From his porch on a neighboring farm, Juan Gerardi heard the first shot and saw the trespassers fleeing Lima's property. The second shot struck Gerardi in the leg. Gerardi has threatened to sue Lima for battery, claiming damages of medical expenses and lost wages. Because Lima is a good shot, she probably could have hit the trespassers had that been her intent. Lima was unaware of Gerardi's location when she fired the shots.

DISCUSSION: Gerardi's battery claim against Lima hinges on the legal issue of the transferability of Lima's intent in causing the harm inflicted upon Gerardi. Although intent to cause harm is an essential element of a battery action, specific intent with regard to the victim of the injury is not required in a tort action for assault and battery. Morrow v. Flores, 225 S.W.2d 621, 623-24 (Tex. Civ. App.—Fort Worth 1949, writ ref'd n.r.e.). Also, intent to cause harm in a tort action is not limited to harm that the actor intended. The actor's intent to cause one harm satisfies the intent requirement for the harm actually resulting from the act. Bennight v. Western Auto Supply Co., 670 S.W.2d 373, 378 Tex. App—Austin 1984, writ ref'd n.r.e.). Requisite intent is an essential element of a battery action.

There are two rules of law applicable to this case. First, intent to cause harm to one person extends the actor's liability to another, unintended recipient of the harm. Morrow, 225 S.W.2d at 624, 625. In Morrow, Mr. Morrow was pursuing an individual who had damaged his property. When he encountered the individual, they scuffled briefly, and the individual attempted to flee. Mr. Morrow, armed with a pistol, shot after the fleeing man, missed him, and struck a bystander in the foot. The court held that Mr. Morrow, in intending to shoot the fleeing individual, demonstrated the intent required for a battery action brought by the unintended recipient of the injury.

13

Similarly, Lima's intent to cause harm, or fear of harm, to the trespassers can be transferred to Gerardi.

The second rule of law deals with the actor's intent to bring about a harm different from the harm intended. An actor's intent to cause harm can be transferred even when the resulting harm is different from the one intended. Bennight, 670 S.W.2d at 377. In Bennight, the manager of a bat-infested auto supply store repeatedly required an employee, whom he knew was apprehensive of the bats, to enter one area. On one such occasion, the employee was bitten by a bat. The question before the court was whether the manager's conduct satisfied the intent requirement of a battery claim. The court held that, even though the manager never intended that the employee actually be bitten, he intentionally placed her in apprehension of being bitten, and this conduct constituted assault. Id. at 379. The court held further that the manager's intention to commit this assault against the employee transferred to her specific injury, even though the manager may not have intended that harm. Id. at 380.

In Bennight, the court held intent transferred when the manager of an auto supply store intended to cause apprehension, but instead caused actual harm. 670 S.W.2d at 378. In our situation, Ms. Lima intended to frighten the trespassers but instead actually harmed Mr. Gerardi. Therefore, the intent element of a battery claim against Lima for causing an unintended harm to an unintended victim should be satisfied.

Lima may argue that she did not intend to harm the two trespassers on her property, and that intent should therefore not be transferred to Gerardi. However, as in Bennight, the facts establish that Lima did intend to cause an apprehension of harm in the two trespassers. By Lima's intentionally causing the trespassers' apprehension, her conduct is analogous to the manager's conduct in Bennight. Although the manager in Bennight did not intend a battery against his employee, he did intentionally place the employee in apprehension of a battery, and this conduct was sufficient to sustain a battery claim. Lima's intent to scare the trespassers constitutes assault, and her intent to commit assault is transferred to the battery that she caused.

Lima's situation is distinguishable from Bennight in that she was attempting to protect her own property. However, there is no evidence that

Lima had any privilege to fire upon these trespassers. Moreover, a court would probably look to the broader policy considerations behind the holdings of <u>Bennight</u> and <u>Morrow</u>. Both cases promote responsibility to the unintended victim of potentially harmful conduct. <u>Morrow</u> makes an actor liable for his actions beyond the intended recipient, while <u>Bennight</u> extends an actor's liability to harm beyond that which is intended. It would be inconsistent with both the holdings and the policy goals of these cases to reduce or eliminate liability when a person commits deliberately harmful acts that result in unintended harm to an unintended victim. Therefore, the intent element of a battery claim against Lima should be satisfied.

Readers should be able to understand the overall legal question and its substantive support—through those topic sentences alone. Here is a list of those sentences, isolated from the text:

1. Gerardi's battery claim against Lima hinges on the legal issue of the transferability of Lima's intent in causing the harm inflicted upon Gerardi.
2. There are two rules of law applicable to this case.
3. The second rule of law deals with the actor's intent to bring about a harm different from the harm intended.
4. In <u>Bennight</u>, the court held intent transferred when the manager of an auto supply store intended to cause apprehension, but instead caused actual harm.
5. Lima may argue that she did not intend to harm the two trespassers on her property, and that intent should therefore not be transferred to Gerardi.
6. Lima's situation is distinguishable from <u>Bennight</u> in that she was attempting to protect her own property.

Read together, the topic sentences form an elliptical but coherent paragraph.

- Topic sentence 1 adequately introduces the overarching issue of the memo, transferability.

- Topic sentence 2 is a useful set-up; a stronger sentence would have also introduced readers to the first rule.
- Topic sentence 3 summarizes the second rule of harm: different from harm intended.
- Topic sentence 4 summarizes <u>Bennight's</u> holding. Perhaps a reference to the case at hand would tie the ideas together better.
- Topic sentence 5 anticipates the counteranalysis from Lima's perspective.
- Topic sentence 6 distinguishes <u>Bennight's</u> facts. This last topic sentence might have offered a conclusion.

Experiment with your rough draft by separating each topic sentence from your text: is each one a strong introduction to or conclusion about that paragraph's main idea? Next, examine the coherence of the topic sentences as they relate to the overall thesis set-up. At this point, you may decide that some added transitions will smooth the reader's path.

TRY THESE

Evaluate the paragraph below for its topic sentence and usefulness. If it is ineffective, rewrite it, organizing the material into logic order.

1. An employer is often limited in ability to accommodate an employee's handicap. "It is not necessary that a new, unneeded position be created but, rather, if a new disability prevents an employee from performing his present job, an effort to place him in an existing position which is vacant and for which he is qualified to perform must be made." [cite] The employer is not required to create positions to accommodate a handicapped employee because that would pose "undue hardship on the conduct of the employer's business." [cite] In <u>Ali v. Chelsea Catering</u>, the court determined that an employer does not fail to accommodate the plaintiff if he does not have any present openings that could be safely filled by the handicapped employee. [cite] The employer is "within its rights to subject the handicapped employee to the full range of disciplinary proceedings up to and including discharge." [cite]

This will be the most difficult element of the prima facie case for the plaintiff to establish. Her performance reviews reflect an inability to match professional standards, and she is unable to perform her job safely. The company will suffer financially if she is retained. No other position is available that has a lower level of physical or mental requirements.

Evaluate this student's introductory paragraph (with road map); then compare it to the student's topic sentences that follow.

2. The court is likely to hold that Donner is not shielded from liability for the automobile accident. The Court of Appeals of the District of Columbia has held that "one who is (1) suddenly stricken by an illness, (2) which he had no reason to anticipate, while driving an automobile, (3) which renders it impossible for him to control the car, is not chargeable with negligence." [Cite.] In the instant case, the principal issue is whether Donner had reason to anticipate his sudden lapses into sleep before the accident occurred.

a. The court is likely to find that Donner had reason to anticipate his sudden lapse into deep sleep.

b. In a case analogous to ours, the driver of an automobile fainted without anticipation, swerved into an embankment, and injured a passenger.

c. Donner's automobile became uncontrollable immediately preceding the accident.

TRANSITIONS

Transitions may look insignificant, but they are one of the few techniques writers have available to facilitate logical connections between ideas. Whether connecting large-scale segments, paragraphs, sentences, or words, transitions signal relationships. Some traditional transitions explain those relationships right up front: *again, once, finally, however.* Other stylistic devices such as repetition and dovetailing (see below) can also act as transitions, gluing ideas together without a specific word transition. As the writer, it is your job to connect words and ideas so that your readers don't have to do the mental work for you.

Your legal readers should be able to trace how you structure your discussions, descriptions, and arguments by focusing on these transitions. A carefully placed "on the other hand" immediately alerts your reader, just as "a similar case" does. Watch how quickly you can skim the following paragraph from a brief, simply by following the transitions.

> ▶ **Under the Establishment Clause**, governmental granting of denominational preferences is regarded as suspect subject to the strictest scrutiny. **Only a com-**
> ▶ **pelling government interest** can serve as justification, and the degree must be narrowly tailored to furthering
> ▶ that interest. **While** the state has a purpose and interest in protecting the health and welfare of minors, the appellate court's order regarding this child's religious exposure was not narrowly drawn to further her best
> ▶ interest. **In fact**, the district court failed to meet the requisite showing of a causal relationship between the religious practice and actual or probable harm to the child. See <u>Kirchner</u>, 606, A.2d at 262.
> ▶ **Instead**, the trial court erroneously **focused on**
> ▶ **three findings** to justify intrusion in establishing the
> ▶ child's religion. **First**, exposure to two conflicting re-
> ▶ ligions causes the child stress. (R. at 8) **Second**, the child has a "positive sense of identity" as a Jew. (R. at
> ▶ 117) **Finally**, the parties had agreed to raise the child as a Jew despite the mother's Christian upbringing. (R. at 218, 77)

> The court should not have imposed its authority on the decision regarding this child's religious training based on **these findings**. The **first two findings** do not meet the required showing that involvement in church
> harms the child. **The third finding** is irrelevant to the required showing of harm, and giving it any weight is in itself a violation of the Establishment Clause. **Thus, by imposing its authority, the court violated the Establishment Clause of the First Amendment.

In addition to these obvious transitions, a careful, deliberate **repetition** of words/ideas can create cohesion, as can **dovetailing** (using words with a similar linguistic base like "deny" and "denial"[2]):

> The concept of "racial discrimination" may be approached from the perspective of either its victim or its
> **perpetrator**. . . . The **perpetrator perspective** presupposes a world composed of atomistic individuals whose actions are outside of and apart from the social fabric and without historical continuity. . . . **It is a**
> **world where**, but for the conduct of these misguided ones, the system of equality of opportunity would work to provide a distribution of the good things in life with-
> out racial disparities and **where** deprivations that did correlate with race would be "deserved" by those deprived on the grounds of "insufficient merit." **It is a**
> **world where** such things as "vested rights," "objective selection systems," and "adventitious decisions" (all of which serve to prevent victims from experiencing any change in conditions) are matters of fate, having **nothing** to do with the problem of racial discrimination.
>
> *Source*: Alan Freeman, Legitimizing Racial Discrimination Through Antidiscrimination Law: A Critical Review of Supreme Court Doctrine, 62 MINN. L. REV. 1049, 1052 (1978) (emphasis added) (citations omitted).

---

[2] See, for instance, Anne Enquist's revealing discussion in The Legal Writing Handbook 565 (1998).

Case names and citation information rarely function as effective topic sentences. When readers begin a paragraph without an effective topic sentence, they cannot assimilate a new case name and citation into your textual flow. Evaluate the reading ease of the following paragraphs:

> . . . Two EEOC factors to consider are duration of impairment and its nature and severity.
>
> In <u>Rogers v. International Marine Terminals, Inc.</u>, 87 F.3d 755 (5th Cir. 1996), the parties agreed that Wade Roger's ankle problems constituted a physical impairment and, therefore, the question before the court was of substantial limitation.

It is difficult to imagine the connection between the second paragraph and the one leading into it. Rather, the sentence's emphasis could have been on the holding.

A simple and equally useful device is an added transition into a new paragraph:

> . . . Two EEOC factors to consider are duration of impairment and its nature and severity.
>
> **If the parties stipulate the severity of injury,** the court can address only the remaining question of its duration. **For instance,** in <u>Rogers v. International Marine Terminals, Inc.</u>, 87 F.3d 755 (5th Cir. 1996), the parties agreed that Wade Roger's ankle problems constituted a physical impairment and, therefore, the question before the court was of substantial limitation.

Special attention is necessary when the paragraph discusses the holdings of two cases, even if the points of the two cases are consistent and supportive:

> . . . In oral employment contracts, the courts have held that neither partial nor full performance will be sufficient to take the contract out of the statute of frauds. <u>Mercer v. C.A. Roberts Co.</u>, 570 F.2d 1232, 1237 (5th Cir. 1978).

Similarly, in <u>Paschall v. Anderson</u>, 91 S.W.2d 1050 (Tex. 1936), the court held that full performance was not enough to take the contract out of the statute of frauds. In <u>Chevalier v. Lane's, Inc.</u>, 213 S.W.2d 530 (Tex. 1948), the court held that part performance is not enough to take an oral contract out of the statute. Later in *Collins v. McCombs*, 511 S.W.2d 745 (Tex. Civ. App.—San Antonio 1974, writ ref'd n.r.e.), the court reaffirmed its stance that full performance will not take an oral employment contract out of the statute of frauds.

The second topic sentence ("Similarly . . .") connects <u>Mercer</u> to <u>Paschall</u> but does not anticipate <u>Chevalier</u>. If both cases are "similar" to <u>Mercer</u>, the topic sentence should point out that <u>Mercer</u> is a culmination of two earlier cases. When you are reworking these cases, you may decide to reorganize along different lines altogether.

There is no "right" or "wrong" way to organize; organization embodies both the audience and the message. Focusing specifically on organization, however, will help your review of your thought process and logic: thesis, road map, headings, topic sentences, and transitions.

Examining Your Organization

Here's a useful tip for examining the organization of your draft: cut the draft into paragraph blocks, scramble the blocks, and reassemble them to their original order using only the topic sentences and transitions. If you have to reread each of your own paragraphs to make your judgment, imagine how difficult it would be for your reader to follow what you are saying! Better return to the draft and sharpen your internal cues.

If you want to tighten your document even more, cut one of your paragraphs into separate sentences, mix up its sentences, and ask a friend to reorganize the paragraph. If your friend can't find the topic sentence and reassemble the original, return to that draft. You're not finished.

TRY THIS

After reviewing the following paragraph, add transitions and dovetailing so that the paragraph has coherence.

Helen Pergene was employed at the New Orleans South High School as a government teacher and audio visual coordinator from 1995 until September 16, 1999. On August 30, 1999, Mrs. Pergene appeared on local television as a spokesperson for "Open Doors," a libertarian organization. Open Doors lobbies for the legal status of alternative familial arrangements. During her television interview, Mrs. Pergene argued for single-sex adoptions and the passage of current legislation. She revealed an internal school memo from the principal. The memo instructed faculty to avoid any mention of the pending legislation.

WHAT TO REMEMBER

Each legal document will have its own requirements for a conclusion. A memorandum, for instance, may require a brief review of both the arguments and counter arguments along with a restatement of your final evaluation. A brief will follow the terms the court has set down, perhaps a separate section or paragraph asking for specific relief based on the restated law. You must use your common sense in a client communication: probably the closing is the spot where you'll list what the client needs to do next or you'll offer your time for another meeting.

CONCLUDING EXERCISES

1. **Thesis and road maps.** Many readers would not be able to follow the road map paragraph below. Why, and how would you correct the problem?

Both Federal Rules of Civil Procedure 26(b)(4)(B) and 26(b)(1) may be applied to determine the discoverability of the identities of persons retained or specifically employed by a party in anticipation of a case that did not expect to be called as witnesses at trial. The two rules will be examined for textual content, the possible intent of the drafters, and policy justifications associated with each.

2. **Road map paragraphs and headings.** Are the headings anticipated? Are they effective?

Mintz's complaint probably fails to meet the specificity requirement required by the Second Circuit for civil rights actions. Generally, federal courts are lenient in accepting pleadings. The Second Circuit, however, has established a specificity requirement for actions involving civil rights, and several Second Circuit cases have discussed and applied this requirement. Some other considerations, however, weigh against the sufficiency of Mintz's request.

• • •

a. The General Rule and the Second Circuit's Specificity Requirement
b. Case Law
c. Counter analysis

3. **Topic sentences and transitions.** Rewrite the following draft paragraph so that readers can anticipate its contents and follow its reasoning.

In <u>Freeman</u>, the court ruled that there was reasonable suspicion because both the store clerk and the store manager witnessed the customer's putting her hand down her shirt while standing at the earring display rack. <u>Freeman v. Kar Way Inc.</u>, 686 So. 2d 53 (La. Ct. App. 1998). In <u>Derouen</u>, an employee witnessed the customer placing a bag of shrimp in her shopping bag and then placing an object in her purse. <u>Derouen v. Miller</u>, 614 So. 2d 1306 (La. Ct. App. 1993). The holdings of these cases were similar. Both courts held that there was reasonable suspicion to detain and question the customer because the act of thievery was witnessed by an employee. In Miss Miller's case, the issue presented is whether the store manager had probable cause to detain Miss Miller under the context of the code.

4. **Transitions.** Review this memorandum's statement of facts and add or change transitions to create coherence.

The store clerk turned to assist a customer. The clerk saw that both Miss Dobrowski and the necklace were gone. The clerk immediately called a manager. The manager saw Miss Dobrowski, who matched the description the clerk gave, and quickly got her attention. He informed Miss Dobrowski that she was a suspect. Miss Dobrowski denied that she had taken anything from the store and refused to go with the manager for questioning. The manager grabbed Miss Dobrowski and detained her in the office. Miss Dobrowski protested loudly as the manager took her through the store. The manager physically placed her in the office and locked the door. The manager left to take care of another incident. He went to find the clerk who had reported the theft. Half an hour later, he returned with the clerk. The clerk could not positively identify Miss Dobrowski. The manager asked Miss Dobrowski to empty her purse. She complied. No jewelry was found. She was allowed to leave the store.

5. **Reviewing a draft.** Return to the student memorandum, p. 12, and add a road map. Strengthen three of the topic sentences.

◆ ◆ ◆

Rewriting is not virtuous. It isn't something that ought to be done.
It is simply something that most writers find they have to do to
discover what they have to say and how to say it.

DONALD MURRAY, LEARNING BY TEACHING:
SELECTED ARTICLES ON WRITING AND TEACHING 69 (1982).

◆ ◆ ◆

2

CREATING SENTENCES WITH STYLE

It's back to your draft for a look at readability: Will your readers understand everything on a first read-through, or are your sentences so long and convoluted that your readers will be forced either to reread or to abandon the project?

It takes most new law students only about a week before they begin producing sentences that resemble those in case books. Capitulating to this subliminal seduction is natural but also counterproductive for novices trying to incorporate new legal concepts into those new and ponderous sentence structures. It's an incorporation doomed to failure. Even if you succeed at reproducing casebook prose, you'll have failed your writing job for your reader.

This chapter examines problems that commonly affect the readability of sentence-level legal prose. The idea here is that you'll return to your now-organized draft and tackle each sentence until it says what you want it to say. That requires time—the same sort of time your future legal documents will also demand.

OVERVIEW

- ◆ Long sentences
- ◆ Front-loaded sentences
- ◆ Awkward citation placement
- ◆ Treacherous placement
- ◆ Faulty parallelism
- ◆ If-then constructions
- ◆ Passives
- ◆ Excessive/intrusive quotations

Using the end of a sentence for emphasis is almost intuitive. Jokes have their punch lines at the end. In mystery stories, we discover the culprit at the end. We like closure. For example, if you were organizing the American Revolution, which rallying cry would you pick:

It is tyranny to tax citizens who are unrepresented!

OR

Taxation without representation is tyranny!

LOUIS SIRICO AND NANCY SCHULTZ, PERSUASIVE WRITING
FOR LAWYERS AND THE LEGAL PROFESSION 29 (1995)

◆ ◆ ◆ ◆

There are only two cures for the long sentence:
(1) Say less;
(2) Put a period in the middle.
Neither expedient has taken hold in the law.
DAVID MELLINKOFF, THE LANGUAGE OF THE LAW 366 (1963)

◆ ◆ ◆ ◆

LONG SENTENCES

Most legal sentences are too long. Open any casebook to a random page and you will find copious examples. Not all short sentences are easier to read (indeed, some are baffling),[1] but a series of long legal sentences requires too much effort for the average reader. Legal sentences are frequently long because legal training is a process of qualifying, narrowing, and delineating with evidence. Thus your new skill at qualifying and delineating can force your essential information into a chain of clauses that becomes long, convoluted sentences.

Not all long sentences are difficult reading, of course; no set number of words or typed lines breaks readability rules. If legal sentences are carefully punctuated and cued, then all those necessary qualifications will not affect the document's readability. Without proper cueing, though, a chain of clauses will confuse readers:

	The Court of Appeals, Cummings,
"that instruction that if"? ▶	Circuit Judge, held **that** instruction
another "that if plaintiff"! ▶	**that if** jury found **that if** plaintiff
	stored property in good condition in
	defendant's warehouse **and** the property was returned in damaged condi-
"recovery"—there's more? ▶	tion, plaintiffs were entitled to recov-
"unless"—here we go again ▶	ery **unless** jury found that defendant
	exercised ordinary care and diligence
"to prevent . . . to explain"—I'm lost. ▶	**to prevent** damage to the property was
"was sufficient"—what's the ▶ subject here?	sufficient to explain Illinois law on
	burden of proof in bailment cases **and,**
"cases" AND?—at least there is a ▶ comma, but wait—a 2-line parenthetical	in absence of instruction that plaintiffs had ultimate burden of proof with
	respect to defendant's fault, defendant
"Defendant was entitled to a ▶ reversal"—should I be glad or sad?	was entitled to a reversal. Celanese
	Corp. of America v. Vandalia
	Warehouse Corp., 424 F.2d 1176 (7th
What did they say? ▶	Cir. 1970) (emphasis added).

---

[1] For instance: A mouse is what is eaten or caught by a trap or a rat. Sounds logical? But how can a trap eat a mouse? For a full discussion of this, and other, drafting problems, see DAVID MELLINKOFF, THE LANGUAGE OF THE UNIFORM COMMERCIAL CODE, 77 EMORY L. REV. 185, 215.

SOLUTIONS

1. Where possible, **break** embedded clauses into separate independent clauses or sentences.

> **✗** In an attempt to mitigate the harshness of this doctrine, the courts developed the idea of constructive eviction **whereby** a tenant could assert **that** the condition of the premises was such **that** they were unlivable **and** therefore he had been "constructively evicted" by his landlord.

Broken into Two Sentences
In an attempt to mitigate the harshness of this doctrine, the courts developed the idea of "constructive eviction." **A** tenant could assert that the condition of the premises was unlivable and therefore **that** he had been "constructively evicted" by his landlord.

Broken into Two Sentences and Transition
A tenant could assert that the condition of the premises was unlivable; **thus,** he follows the court-created idea that he was "constructively evicted" by his landlord.

2. Avoid excessive coordination and subordination.

> **✗** If the neighbor has caused pecuniary loss **or** substantial inconvenience to the Company **or** a third person, *this cause is available* **if** the **neighbor has,** without the effective consent of the Company, intentionally **or** knowingly **tampered** with its tangible property.

This cause is available (1) **if** the **neighbor has** intentionally or knowingly **tampered** with the Company's tangible property without the effective consent of the Company and (2) **if** the neighbor has caused pecuniary loss or substantial inconvenience to the Company or a third person.

3. Place the **subject close to the verb**, and place both of them toward the beginning of the sentence.

> **X** The first issue is whether **representations** made by Julius Getman regarding Louisiana's future plans to eliminate the student environmental clinic **meet** the requirements of fraud and negligent misrepresentation.

The first issue is whether Julius Getman's **representations meet** the requirements of fraud and negligent misrepresentation. **Getman represented** Louisiana's future plans to eliminate the student environmental clinic.

4. If the sentence length is absolutely necessary, then add **signposts:**

   a. Add **word signposts**.
   b. **Punctuate** to allow for closure.
   c. **Tabulate** parallel lists and ideas.

ADD SIGNPOSTS. Careful **signposting** can help defeat necessarily long sentences. Words can be signposts when they signal relationships: transitions, repetitions of words or phrases, introductions, and conclusions.

The following paragraph incorporates enough signposting that the prose compels readers into and through it:

> **Nothing** that is worth doing can be achieved in our lifetime; *therefore*, we must be *saved by* hope. **Nothing** which is true or beautiful or good makes complete sense in any immediate context of history; *therefore* we must be *saved by* faith. **Nothing** we do, however virtuous, can be accomplished alone; *therefore* we are saved by love. **No** virtuous act is quite as virtuous from the standpoint of our friend or foe as it is from our standpoint. *Therefore* we must be *saved by* the favor of love which is forgiveness.
>
> Reinhold Niebuhr,
> *The Irony of American History 36 (1952)*

PUNCTUATION SIGNPOSTS. In addition to words used as signposts, **punctuation signposts** can make the message more accessible, as the following colon illustrates:

> The Comptroller cannot be bound to follow the erroneous advice of his agent for two reasons: The taxpayer has the burden of proving the affirmative advice was affirmatively given, and the taxpayer must show that the agent was aware of all the circumstances and yet advised him on an erroneous course of taxable action.

NUMBERED LISTS (TABULATION). Finally, you can also use **numbered lists (tabulation)** to create an organizational hierarchy (and add white space to the page). The following example, from an attorney's client letter, suffers from both length and embedded clauses, but we can revise it by adding tabulation.

> **X** When respondents are questioned by suspicious interviewers, subjects tend to view their responses as deceptive even when they are honest, which significantly increases errors in detection of honesty. Two distinct phenomena contribute to these errors: the suspicious interrogation distorts observers' perceptions, and the interrogation causes stress for the respondent, which in turn induces behavior likely to be interpreted as deceptive. This latter phenomenon has been called the "Othello's error," since Othello mistook Desdemona's distress and despair in response to his accusation of infidelity.

Revision

When respondents are questioned by suspicious interviewers, subjects tend to view their responses as deceptive even when they are honest, which significantly increases errors in detection of honesty. Two distinct phenomena contribute to these errors:

1. the suspicious interrogation distorts observers' perceptions, and
2. the interrogation causes stress for the respondent, which in turn induces behavior likely to be interpreted as deceptive.

This latter phenomenon has been called the "Othello's error," since Othello mistook Desdemona's distress and despair in response to his accusation of infidelity.

Thus, as you sharpen your draft, you can use signpost words, **punctuation,** and tabulation to help your readers understand necessarily long sentences.

Either (1) justify leaving the following sentences at their current length or (2) create a more understandable sentence: break into separate sentences, punctuate for clarity, signpost, position subject and verb closer together, tabulate.

1. A Cuban journalist has been jailed for four years, dissident sources and the international press freedom watchdog group Reporters Without Borders said.

2. <u>Klopps v. Adonis</u>, unlike the kind of in rem action typified by <u>Harris v. Balk</u>, 198 U.S. 215 (1905), in which the property attached was an intangible debt owed by one person to another, involves a tangible form of property.

3. With proper rules, the nonstatutory breed registries (e.g., Appaloosa, Arabian, etc.) could lose their registry status or have their animals barred from pari-mutuel competitions if their members and registered animals are regularly involved in unregistered meets or illegal activities related to racing.

4. In the event of a default on a payment, the entire amount of an employer's withdrawal liability plus accrued interest on the total outstanding liability from the due date of the first payment which was not timely made becomes due immediately. 29 U.S.C. § 1399(c)(5).

◆ ◆ ◆ ◆

Good editing requires reading the document as if you've never seen it before; that is hard to do if you have been working on it intensely. Try to arrive at the editing stage with enough time to put the document down for at least a day. Even if you do not have that luxury, let at least a couple hours pass; then try to read as if you were a complete stranger to the document.
LINDA HOLDEMAN EDWARDS, LEGAL WRITING 217 (1996).

◆ ◆ ◆ ◆

FRONT-LOADED SENTENCES

Sentences that place qualifying or descriptive information before the main subject and its verb are "front-loaded." If you create these lopsided sentences, your readers will find it hard to process the introductory, dependent material before they have a context for it; they'll have to read through it, hold it in abeyance, and then find some way to put those introductory words into context:

> **X** Based upon a review of the material regarding the Worker's Compensation Joint Insurance Fund that resulted in the Agency's granting of an exemption for a similar fund in 1984 and the material submitted by the expert at our meeting, in my opinion the above-captioned **funds meet** the requirements for exemption as a government entity organization.

This sentence places 39 words before the beginning of the main clause—and the main subject is *hidden* behind "in my opinion." When you review your draft searching for ways to sharpen your prose, make sure the subjects of your sentences are placed near the beginning.

SOLUTIONS

1. **Break up** a front-loaded sentence into two sentences.

   The above-captioned **funds meet** the requirements for exemption as a government entity organization. **This opinion** is based upon a review of the material regarding the Worker's Compensation Joint Insurance Fund that resulted in the Agency's granting of an exemption for a similar fund in 1984 and the material submitted by the expert at our meeting.

2. Flip-flop the sentence so that the main subject and verb are first.

The above-captioned **funds meet** the requirements for exemption as a government entity organization, **which is my opinion** based upon a review of the material regarding the Worker's Compensation Joint Insurance Fund that resulted in the Agency's granting of an exemption for a similar fund in 1984 and the material submitted by the expert at our meeting.

A bit of strategy: You may find a front-loaded sentence useful if you need to hide your true message.

TRY THESE

Experiment with flip-flopping and then breaking these front-loaded sentences. Which rewrite reads more smoothly?

1. If the juror and the defendant are of the same socio-economic class, or if the juror is in a higher class than the defendant, depending on the voir dire and the nature of the case, perhaps the juror will be more sympathetic and more disposed to give the defendant a break.

2. After the Commission's general counsel noted that the District would have the opportunity to contest the necessity for the proposed halfway house at the upcoming hearing on its application for an amendment to its halfway housing permits, the Commission accepted the District's application.

◆ ◆ ◆ ◆

**Style is the difference between getting your ideas
written and getting your ideas read by someone else.**
Overheard at a Continuing Legal Education Program

◆ ◆ ◆ ◆

AWKWARD CITATION PLACEMENT

To sharpen the prose of your draft, you must focus on the placement of your citations. Citations are necessary, important, and generally compact, but they can intrude on the point you want to make and impede your reader's comprehension. Citations document legal points. Do not let their location in your sentences obscure your substantive message.

X Sadler v. Musicland-Pickwick Int'l, Inc., 31 Fed. R. Serv. 2d (Callaghan) 760 (E.D. Tex. 1980), narrowed the test to "relative difficulty" and repetition of steps by both parties.

X Complete diversity of citizenship must exist between parties. Strawbridge v. Curtiss, 7 U.S. 267 (1806). Gordon v. Steele, 376 F. Supp. 575 (W.D. Pa. 1974), held that it is citizenship at the time of filing suit that is controlling.

Of course, citation placement is not citation deletion. No legal reader could accept as accurate an argument without documentation, so you don't want to omit the citation altogether just to avoid graceless citation placement. Rather, you want the grace and message of your point to be supported by the citation.

SOLUTIONS

1. Move citations into prepositional phrases.

The court, in Sadler v. Musicland-Pickwick Int'l, Inc., 31 Fed. R. Serv. 2d (Callaghan) 760 (E.D. Tex. 1980), narrowed the test to "relative difficulty" and repetition of steps by both parties.

2. Move citations to the end of your sentence.

A federal court narrowed the test to "relative difficulty" and repetition of steps by both parties. <u>Sadler v. Musicland-Pickwick Int'l, Inc.</u>, 31 Fed. R. Serv. 2d (Callaghan) 760 (E.D. Tex. 1980).

3. Avoid ending one sentence with a citation and beginning the next sentence with another citation.

The 1806 Supreme Court announced that complete diversity of citizenship must exist between parties. <u>Strawbridge v. Curtiss</u>, 7 U.S. 267 (1806). In 1974, however, a Pennsylvania court held that it is citizenship at the time of filing suit that is controlling. <u>Gordon v. Steele</u>, 376 F. Supp. 575 (W.D. Pa. 1974).

A final note: Citation abbreviations are forms of documentation and NOT part of the text. As the Harvard Manual on Style explains, a citation used as a noun in a textual sentence is technically incorrect. The abbreviation is correct within a citation entry, but it is NOT correct as a noun within a sentence.[2]

Move or correct the following citations using the above suggestions.

1. <u>Atkins v. Kirkpatrick</u>, 832 S.W.2d 547 (Tenn. Ct. App. 1991), set forth four standards necessary for "negligent misrepresentation."

2. The case is governed by La. Code Crim. Proc. Ann. Art 215 (West 1987).

3. Even a single wheat farmer's decision to plant his own crop was held to fall under the third category of interstate commerce regulation, <u>Wickard v. Filburn</u>, 317 U.S. 111 (1942), so that Congress was empowered to regulate his activity.

4. 29 U.S.C. § 1399(b)(2)(A)(i) allows the employer to seek review of the schedule of payments; however, this dispute also falls under § 1401, the arbitration provision.

---

[2] *See* THE BLUEBOOK: A UNIFORM SYSTEM OF CITATION Rule 10.2.1(c) (16th Ed. 1996).

◆ ◆ ◆

Eight percent of married men cheat in America.
(The rest cheat in Europe.)

◆ ◆ ◆

TREACHEROUS PLACEMENT

Serious consequences develop in legal writing if words aren't placed exactly where they need to be—and also if a word could modify more than one antecedent. When you examine your draft, concentrate on which words you intend to belong together as a unit, and which words you've placed where they might describe more than one noun.

Look, for instance, at the simple word "only." The internal logic of the word requires it to modify or emphasize the word immediately following it. By examining the variety of sentence meaning created in the example below, you realize that writers can unwittingly produce major problems if they slide the word even one place too far.

He shot himself in the foot Monday.
Only **he** shot himself in the foot Monday.
He *only* **shot** himself in the foot Monday.
He shot *only* **himself** in the foot Monday.
He shot himself *only* **in the foot** Monday.
He shot himself in the foot *only* **Monday**.
He shot himself in the foot Monday *only*.

A second interesting example of placement problems comes with the introductory adverb "however." Linguists understand that writers have the same freedom to place "however" as they do any other introductory adverbs like "nevertheless," "moreover," etc.[3] Its placement

---

[3] Many legal writers agreed with Strunk and White that "however" should not begin a sentence unless it means "in whatever way" or "to whatever extent"; e.g., "However you talk to him, he will still believe you are angry." WILLIAM STRUNK, JR. & E.B. WHITE, THE ELEMENTS OF STYLE 49 (3d ed. 1979). This suggestion can aid certain sentences, but it does not limit the placement of "however."

should emphasize intended emphasis or contrast. Watch what happens with a sentence from Stephen Carter's CIVILITY 284 (1998):

> If lawyers are paid to be rude and political consultants to be nasty, then professional athletes surely can brawl and bite the ears of their opponents. **After all**, athletes want to win too.

> If lawyers are paid to be rude and political consultants to be nasty, then professional athletes surely can brawl and bite the ears of their opponents. Athletes, **after all**, want to win too.

> If lawyers are paid to be rude and political consultants to be nasty, then professional athletes surely can brawl and bite the ears of their opponents. Athletes want to win too, **after all**.

Each option emphasizes something different and is not wrong, but one placement may best suit your meaning.

A sentence with a *modifier* and two or more nouns may confuse the reader:

 I own an *old* computer and printer.

As written, the sentence's computer is definitely old; the printer **may also** be old. "May be," however, is not concise enough for legal readers; precise modification is essential. Daily, courts are forced to interpret contract clauses with modifiers floating among several nouns; daily, lawyers argue over statutes and codes because the drafter did not precisely place the modifier.

SOLUTIONS

1. As you examine your draft, carefully **evaluate** each modifier to find any modifying word or phrase that might be interpreted to modify more than one noun.

    The candidate must pass the written test and the durability test within one week before beginning work. (must take durability test within a week; might also have to take written test within a week—but it's ambiguous)

Add Comma
The candidate must pass the written test and the durability test, within one week before beginning work. (must do both within one week)

Move to Modify Full Clause
Within one week of beginning work, the candidate must pass the written test and the durability test. (must do both within one week)

Revise Syntax
The candidate must pass the written test within one week of beginning work and the durability test, also within one week of beginning work. (must do both within one week; rather repetitive here)

2. If you intend the modifier to limit only one noun within the sentence, then **break the sentence** in two or add additional limitations to the antecedents.

Broken into Two Sentences
The candidate must, within one week before beginning work, pass the written test. He also must pass the durability test.

Separated Antecedents and "Also"
The candidate must pass the written test within one week before beginning work, and he should also pass the durability test.

3. The best strategy for avoiding modifier muddle is to slowly and systematically **review** your drafts, **searching** for any sentence in which your modifiers could have misinterpreted antecedents.

TRY THESE

Examine the placement of modifiers in these sentences. If they are misplaced or ambiguous, correct them. If they represent two or more interpretations, be prepared to explain those possibilities.

1. Christi Mayhem tried "at least ten times" to leave Cornelius Fenwick, father of her two baby boys, who she said would beat her regularly.

2. Article 2.11 (B) only requires diligence to be used to locate the registered agent at the registered address.

3. He claims the psychiatrist, however, contradicted himself during the competency hearing by stating affirmatively that Porter was competent to stand trial.

◆ ◆ ◆

Only as we tumble our words onto the page or into a dictating machine do we begin to see our story, our argument, take shape. The time to focus on the relationships between the disparate parts of our document is during the reading of the first draft. Only then can we see that point one is independent of point two, but that points three and four are inexorably tied to the outcome of point two and thus dependent.

TERRI LeCLERCQ, EXPERT LEGAL WRITING 60 (1995)

◆ ◆ ◆

FAULTY PARALLELISM

Parallel ideas are often forcefully conveyed in parallel grammatical structures. Verbs can be parallel, as can nouns, adjectives—indeed, full sentences. When properly executed, parallel structures frequently produce persuasive, memorable prose.

Say that I was a drum major for justice. Say that I was a drum major for peace. That I was a drum major for righteousness. And all of the other shallow things will not matter.

Martin Luther King, Jr.

Parallel structure can also drive home a point. Look, for instance, at a series of paragraphs Mitch Albom uses to describe his professor's gradual loss of abilities, and imagine how you could repeat this device for your own assignments:

He backed the car out of the garage one morning and could barely push the brakes. That was the end of his driving.

He kept tripping, so he purchased a cane. That was the end of his walking free.

. . . He hired his first home care worker . . . who helped him in and out of the pool, and in and out of his bathing suit. In the locker room, the other swimmers pretended not to stare. That was the end of his privacy.

. . . [to his college class] "I have been teaching this course for twenty years . . . I have a fatal illness. I may not live to finish the semester. If you feel this is a problem, I understand if you wish to drop the course." He smiled.

And that was the end of his secret.

Mitch Albom
Tuesdays with Morrie 8-9 (1997)

Careful use of parallelism, like the "that was the end of . . ." (above), can create memorable prose; misuse of it can create confusion. You might lose parallelism in a list of items because you begin that list with an introductory word or phrase that you later *omitted* from the other parallel words or phrases. Or, you might lose that parallel because your list of items begins not with an omitted word but with an inadvertent *repetition* of the introductory signal.

SOLUTIONS

1. Keep **syntactically equal** items parallel.

 Koby's interaction with the Human Rights Commission included **doing inventory** of past issues and **assistance** about current European cases.

Koby's interaction with the Human Rights Commission included **doing inventory** of past issues and **assisting with** current European cases.

2. Review your **numbered lists,** which must also contain grammatically parallel items.

 Other provisions of Section 6 provide (1) for the requisites of the application for a bondsman's license, (2) for an investigation and hearing by the board, and (3) its denial of the application or approval conditioned on the applicant's filing of the required security deposit.

Other provisions of Section 6 provide (1) for the requisites of the application for a bondsman's license, (2) for an investigation and hearing by the board, and (3) **for** its denial of the application or approval conditioned on the applicant's filing of the required security deposit.

3. Keep **signals** apparent to reflect the parallel.

 Thus, the court held that the complaint was not vague or conclusory and it was "adequate to give notice of the claims asserted."

Thus, the court held **that** the complaint was not vague or conclusory and **that** it was "adequate to give notice of the claims asserted."

4. Avoid losing parallelism with **an inadvertent repetition** of "that" in a string of clauses.

> ✗ He said **that** because he was going to file before June **that** the statute of limitations would not have run.

He said that, because he was going to file before June, the statute of limitations would not have run.

5. Keep items following **correlative conjunctions** parallel.

> ✗ The police officers were looking **neither for** the waitress **nor** the donut-eater, but the two rushed outside to identify themselves. (emphasizes **for**)

> either . . . or
> neither . . . nor
> both . . . and
> not only . . . but also

The police officers were looking **for neither** the waitress **nor** the donut-eater, but the two rushed outside to identify themselves.

> ✗ **Not only** were the freshman students afraid of the new professors **but also** their classmates. (emphasizes **were the freshman students**)

The freshman students were afraid **not only** of the new professors **but also** of their classmates.

TRY THESE

Redo these sentences as necessary to create parallel items within them.

1. It is the type of bureaucratic abuse that, unless someone complains about it, that is going to continue.

2. The plaintiff must show:

    a. a reasonable probability that the parties would enter into a contractual relationship;

    b. that the defendant acted maliciously by intentionally preventing the relationship from occurring with the purpose of harming the plaintiff;

    c. the defendant was not privileged or justified; and

    d. actual harm or damage occurred as a result of the interference.

3. Training first-year instructors plus advertising and interviewing new instructors is a major institutional expense.

◆ ◆ ◆

Anyone who reads a footnote in a judicial opinion would answer a
knock at his hotel door on his wedding night.
DEAN BURTON S. LAMB
DICKINSON LAW SCHOOL, *Quoted by* RUGGERO J. ALDISERT,
177 OPINION WRITING (1990).

◆ ◆ ◆

IF-THEN CONSTRUCTIONS

Sentence structure can expose faulty if-then logic. Review your draft to locate each of your if-then consequences: will readers understand the relationship your logical mind intuitively understands?

> ✗ **If** the broker knew or reasonably believed that the instruments purchased were suitable, **assuming** that the broker knew the investor's objectives, **and when** the broker, with scienter, made material representations relating to the suitability of the instruments, the investor can prevail on a claim of unsuitability **because** she relied, to her detriment, on that fraudulent conduct of the broker.

The investor can prevail on a claim of unsuitability **if** she can establish

43

1. that the broker knew or reasonably believed that the instruments purchased were suitable given the investor's objectives;

2. that the broker, with scienter, made material representations relating to the suitability of the instruments; and

3. that the investor justifiably relied, to her detriment, on the broker's fraudulent conduct.

SOLUTIONS

1. Isolate the conditions from the consequences and search for those **verbal cues that signal** the if-then thought pattern.

   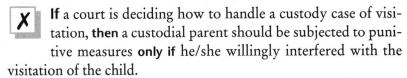 **If** a court is deciding how to handle a custody case of visitation, **then** a custodial parent should be subjected to punitive measures **only if** he/she willingly interfered with the visitation of the child.

   When a court decides how to handle a custody case of visitation, a custodial parent should be subjected to punitive measures **only if** he/she willingly interfered with the visitation of the child.

2. If the **"if" clause defines** who or what the "then" applies to, then start the sentence with "if" to aid readers.

   If the person is from out of state, **then that applicant** must file an additional statement explaining why he or she is entitled to the food stamps.

3. If you have only one "if" clause but **more than one "then,"** then you should (1) start with the "if" and (2) tabulate the "thens."

   If you are caught plagiarizing in law school, then

   1. your professor must report it to the Honor Committee,
   2. the Honor Committee will determine guilt or innocence,
   3. your record will reflect any guilty charge, and
   4. you will be placed on probation or suspension.

4. **Reverse the order** and begin with the "then" clauses if (1) you have more than one "thens" or (2) you want to emphasize the consequence.

Under the proposed statute, **an at-risk child can be removed** from the environment **if** an investigating agent or court determines that the parent or caregiver neglects the child's physical welfare, the home shows evidence of accumulated filth or environmental hazard, there is evidence of physical abuse by someone in the household, or the parents or caregiver openly uses or deals in illegal drugs.

5. If you need more than one "if" and "then" clauses and are concerned that the information is complex, then **break** the sentence or **tabulate** or even create a table.

If you (a) use another student's work as your own, (b) download information from the Internet and fail to document its source, (c) take published words from another's work without documenting its source, or (d) change a few words into paraphrase but do not document your source, then

1. your professor must report it to the Honor Committee,
2. the Honor Committee will determine guilt or innocence,
3. your record will reflect any guilty charge, and
4. you will be placed on probation or suspension.

6. Make sure both the "if" and "when" **modify the proper sentence element.**

> **X**   If the bank is able to prove its prima facie case, the burden **then** shifts to its employee.

If the bank is able to prove its prima facie case, **then** the burden shifts to its employee.

7. Use the **actual words** "if" and "then" rather than substitutes.

> **X**   The issue is **whether**, under Tennessee law, plaintiffs' claim of fraud raises genuine issues of material fact to overcome a defense Motion For Summary Judgment **when** the plaintiffs were induced to sign a lease having been promised the addition of a convenience store, which was later revoked.

45

TRY THESE

Revise these examples so that the logic of the "if-then" is obvious.

1. To constitute fraud or be a ground of rescission, there must not only be a representation as to an existing fact but that representation must have been false; it must have been relied on, and it must have been so material that it determined the conduct of the party seeking relief.

2. If a Louisiana store manager detains the customer without probable cause, detains the customer for over an hour, or uses unnecessary bodily force causing injury, a customer has a cause of action for false imprisonment.

3. If detention is warranted, a merchant, if there is no additional reasonable cause, must end the detention as soon as possible.

◆ ◆ ◆ ◆

The passive was condemned by high school teachers,
grudgingly overlooked by professors, and relied on completely
by law students creating memoranda.

◆ ◆ ◆ ◆

PASSIVE VOICE

We've all been taught to avoid the passive voice, but a rare few of us remember what it is. A quick review: a verb is "active" when the subject of the sentence is performing the action: "The court held that the defendant was negligent." But if the subject is acted upon by something else (as this very clause demonstrates), the verb is "passive":[4] "the plaintiff was injured by the vehicle."

---

[4] Students might confuse the passive voice with a past tense: *The attorney had defended this client. (not passive, merely past perfect tense)* Other writers confuse "to be," used as a linking verb, with the passive voice: *Clark and Lois are preparing today's brief. (active, linking verb—not a passive)* Even the passive voice can have several tenses: *The campaign is being run by the Democrats at Large. (passive, present progressive); The unsuspecting client was hit by an enormous bill. (passive, past tense).* Remember that although the passive voice always includes a form of the "to be" verb, not all "to be" verbs are passive.

Overuse or inadvertent use of the passive voice causes several problems:

- The passive adds unnecessary words.
- The passive steals the punch from strong, active verbs.
- The passive can create ambiguity (truncated passive).
- The passive can misplace sentence emphasis.

Adding unnecessary words:

 The term "cosmic detachment" is used by Richard Wydick to explain abstract legal style. (14 words)

Richard Wydick describes abstract legal style as "cosmic detachment." (9 words)

Stealing the punch from strong, active verbs:

 The plaintiff was severely hurt by the defendant's car.

The defendant's car crippled (paralyzed, injured) the plaintiff.

Adding ambiguity: truncated passives (person/agent missing):

 The pedestrian *was hit* twice. (the subject did not perform the action and the verb has no direct object)

The defendant's car *hit* the pedestrian twice. (the subject, "car," did the hitting)

Gerry Jones, defendant, *hit* the pedestrian twice with his car. (Gerry Jones did the hitting)

Misplacing emphasis:

 In <u>Jabrowski</u> the defendant's plane was flown low over the plaintiff's land during the crop-dusting operation. (Who did what to whom?)

47

In <u>Jabrowski</u> the pilot flew his plane low over the plaintiff's land during the crop-dusting operation.

Artful use of passive voice:

The passive voice can be used deliberately:
- when you *do not know* the agent/actor.
  The girl was propelled out of the train.
- when you need to *protect* your "subject" from a direct accusation.
  Marta was dismissed from law school.
- when you want to *emphasize the result* of an action.
  George was murdered by a drunken driver.

TRY THESE

Switch the following passive constructions into the active voice.

1. The file was misplaced through secretarial error.

2. The right to trial by jury in administrative license revocation proceedings was recently considered by this court in <u>Adams v. Texas State Board of Chiropractic Examiners</u>, 744 S.W.2d 648 (Tex. App.—Austin 1988, no writ).

3. During a hearing outside the presence of a jury on the Defendant's motion to suppress the identification testimony, it was established that Mrs. Brown was currently on deferred adjudication probation for theft over $200.00. [from a probation officer's testimony].

Evaluate the following sentences to decide if recasting the verb into the active voice would strengthen the sentences.

4. The loan was approved by the Lincoln Bank Board of Directors and was on file as an official record of the depository institution.
Leave passive _____ Strengthen with active _____

5. This theme was broadened by the United States Supreme Court in <u>Tully v. Griffin, Inc.</u>, where it was held by the Court that a federal court is "under an equitable duty" to not interfere with a state's collection of its revenue except when "an asserted federal right might otherwise be lost." Leave passive _____ Strengthen with active _____

◆ ◆ ◆ ◆

"[A]uthorities will sometimes seem to have accumulated
without necessity or use, and perhaps will be found, which
might, without loss, to have been omitted."
SAMUEL JOHNSON, PREFACE TO THE DICTIONARY

◆ ◆ ◆ ◆

EXCESSIVE/INTRUSIVE QUOTATIONS

Legal writing is filled with quoted material that interrupts the flow of the text. Yes, our legal system is built on stare decisis and depends on precedent, and yes, the reader needs to know your source. But as you review your draft, evaluate **how much** precedent you've directly quoted and **why**. Were you rushed for time? Was the language too complicated for you to paraphrase?

Huge blocks of quoted information cannot logically address **your** main point. If you include a long block quotation, you cannot simultaneously explain how all of its points fit together with your case. Instead, you resort to

 introducing the connection to your text before you add the block quotation (a rare strategy), or

 concluding with a belated explanation of all the connections, or

 underlining the essential language.

Some writers, of course, cut and paste and then expect readers to create their own connections. Examine the following paragraph, the beginning of a section of a brief, to see this strategy's impact on the reader.

In <u>Allridge v. Scott</u>, 41 F.3d 213, 222 n.12 (5th Cir. 1994), the court noted:

> <u>Simmons</u> particularly applies to those cases in which the state argues that the defendant is a future danger to free society. But when the state argues that the defendant poses a future danger to everybody, fellow inmates included, then <u>Simmons</u> is inapplicable because whether the defendant is eligible for parole is irrelevant.

In <u>Simmons</u>, the defendant was a particular danger to elderly women. <u>Simmons</u>, 114 S.Ct. at 2190.

The 1994 Fifth Circuit found that <u>Simmons</u> has limited application. <u>Allridge v. Scott</u>, 41 F.3d 213, 222 n.12 (5th Cir. 1994). The court determined that <u>Simmons</u> will apply when the state argues that the defendant is a future danger to free society. However, <u>Simmons</u> will be inapplicable if the state argues that the defendant "poses a future danger to everybody, fellow inmates included," because whether the defendant is eligible for parole is irrelevant. In <u>Simmons</u>, the defendant was a particular danger to elderly women. <u>Simmons</u>, 114 S.Ct. at 2190.

Long block quotations:

Pro	Con
■ can fit the important language into a larger context	■ are easily skipped by hurried readers
■ add validity through context of language	■ can be difficult to integrate into a writer's textual point
■ stand out on the page	■ can introduce extraneous material and even contradict the writer's intended point
■ can highlight extended controversial/colorful language	■ can create a black, dense look to a document
	■ can be interpreted as sloppy writing

continues

Con

- need an especially strong introductory tag line and conclusion in the writer's text
- reproduce poorly written prose of the original writer whose point is useful but whose prose is deadly

Shorter word/phrase quotations:

Pro:

- integrate more easily into the writer's text
- will keep the readers' focus on the writer's text rather than on other cases
- allow a writer to keep that part of a holding that is colorful and controversial language in the original that readers could find persuasive

Con:

- if used out of context, can destroy credibility

Paraphrasing:

Pro:

- most successfully integrates outside information into a writer's own text
- creates shorter, smoother documents

Con:

- requires the writer to be more sophisticated with, and take more care to provide, careful signals
- should not be used when the exact wording is in dispute
- can fail if signals indicating who said what are too weak for readers to follow
- can confuse readers if writer quotes more than one source within a sentence

TRY THESE

Rewrite the following sentences so that they read smoothly and correctly, adding or removing punctuation as needed.

1. In <u>Scott v. United States</u>, 79 U.S. (12 Wall.) 443, 445, 20 L. Ed. 438 (1970), the Supreme Court stated:

   > . . . If a contract be unreasonable and unconscionable, but not void for fraud, a court of law will give to the party who sues for its breach damages, not according to its letter, but only such as he is equitably entitled to. . . . [cite]

   Since we have never adopted or rejected such a rule, the question here is actually one of first impression.

2. Under Florida law, prejudgment interest is proper in a specific performance decree. Defendants rely on <u>Town of Longboat Key v. Carl E. Widell & Son</u>, 362 So. 2d 719 (Fla. Dist. Ct. App. 1978), to claim that when damages are not liquidated until time of judgment, the claim is one for unliquidated damages and prejudgment interest must be denied. As noted in <u>Hurley v. Slingerland</u>, 480 So. 2d 104, 107 (Fla. Dist. Ct. App. 1985), the Florida Supreme Court has discredited the test espoused in <u>Town of Longboat</u> by adopting the test that a claim becomes liquidated and susceptible of prejudgment interest *where the trial court's order fixes the amounts due as of specific dates*, citing <u>Argonaut Ins. Co. v. May Plumbing Co.</u>, 474 So. 2d 212 (Fla. 1985).

3. A.S. 25.05.011 defines marriages in Alaska as a "civil contract entered into by one man and one woman that requires both a license and a solemnization."

WHAT TO REMEMBER

A draft is, simply, Step One. Save enough time to edit your draft's organization (with its thesis, roadmap, and headings) and investigate your sentence-level prose: sentence length and order, passives and left-handed sentences, parallel structures, and placement of citations. Reviewing sentences merely as sentences—and not as information-carriers—allows you to see your writing as your reader will: sentence by sentence. Tightening each sentence will give you credibility with your reader and will reduce the length of your draft.

CONCLUDING EXERCISES

Grade yourself on these concluding quizzes that mix the problems you've just reviewed. You'll find possible answers in the Appendix.

Sentence Quiz 1

1. Since defendant G & E may be entitled to qualified immunity from a 28 U.S.C. § 1983 civil action, it must be determined whether defendant G & E conduct violated any clearly established statutory or constitutional right.

2. Where the district court has failed to provide reasons for its decision to deny an indigent civil litigant's request for counsel, the court of appeals in some cases may have to remand, for without the district court's reasons, the appellate court may not be able to determine whether the district court made a reasoned and informed decision regarding the appointment of counsel. [if/then; because/since; for/preposition]

3. This Court's statement in the earlier order that it had received the Defendant's Reply which contained the first fraud-on-the-court argument is certainly some indication that it was considered.

4. Quasi-in-rem jurisdiction was first based on the conceptual basis of state sovereignty. Pennoyer v. Neff, 95 U.S. 714 (1878), held that a state has sovereign power over property and persons within its borders, and over nothing outside of them. Thus a state could legitimately require a nonresident to come into the state to defend a cause of action, or forfeit his forum property. Shaffer v. Heitner, 433 U.S. 186 (1977), held that all assertions of state court power must meet standards of due process as articulated in another Supreme Court case, International Shoe v. Washington, 326 U.S. 310 (1945).

5. Female applicants were asked about plans for future children. Male applicants were not, however.

6. Other provisions of Section 6 provide for the requisites of the application for a bondsman's license, for an investigation and hearing by the board, and its denial of the application or approval conditioned on the applicant's filing of the required security deposits.

7. By losing sight of the "delicate interweaving of the child's developmental tasks with the entangled web of parental conflict" and by imposing changes in custody and access arrangements on ill-equipped children, parents frustrate their children and make them feel helpless.

8. The court can force a child to visit the noncustodial parent only after the judge has (1) afforded parties a hearing, (2) created a proper court order based on findings of fact and conclusions of law, and (3) made findings that include incarceration of a parent if it is reasonably necessary for the welfare of the child.

9. This obligation is not dependent upon Border's intention to submit to arbitration, but rather is imposed on the [c]orporation under the [statute]. ILGWU Nat'l Retirement Fund v. Levy Bros. Frocks, 846 F.2d 859, 885 (2d Cir. 1988); Teamsters Pension Trust Fund v. Allyn Transp. Co., 832 F.2d 502 (9th Cir. 1987).

10. Our client was caught during a robbery. She is not guilty of kidnapping because "Kidnapping is the unlawful movement by physical force of a person against his will and without his consent for a substantial distance where such movement is not merely incidental to the commission of the robbery and where such

movement substantially increases the risk of significant physical injuries to such person over and above those in which such person is normally exposed in the commission of the crime of robbery itself." <u>Roland v. Borg</u>, No. 93-56111, 1994 WL 383840 (9th Cir. 1994).

Sentence Quiz 2

1. A 1977 court found the custodial mother in contempt despite the children's claims that they refused to visit with their father because he abused them and thus declared that the ultimate responsibility rests with the custodial parent who cannot escape his/her duty to comply with the provisions of the decree by attempting to shift the burden to the discretion of her children.

2. The general rule as discussed in <u>Anderson v. McBurney</u>, 467 N.W.2d 158, 160 (Wis. Ct. App. 1991); <u>Brown v. LaChance</u>, 477 N.W.2d 296, 300 (Wis. Ct. App. 1991), is that an attorney cannot be held liable to third parties for acts committed within the scope of attorney-client relationship, absent fraud or negligence in the drafting of an estate planning document. This exception has been narrowly construed by the courts of Wisconsin, which have held it valid in a limited context.

3. Agent further acknowledges that Owner will only accept financing of the sale through one of the four following methods.

4. The plaintiff was not hindered in the prosecution of his case because he was confined, nor was he forbidden access to legal documents.

5. It was thus impossible to determine if the conduct was protected by the first amendment, and under the <u>Nearich</u> test, the allegations were insufficient.

6. Assessing the evidence presented in light most favorable to Aziz, and notwithstanding his having failed to establish the "serious" nature of his injury through expert witness, the facts did not establish the "deliberate indifference" standard required in 42 U.S.C. § 1983.

7. The main reason that the strikers did not cross the picket lines was that they wanted to show solidarity to the management.

8. Case law reasons that a jury informed of the possibility of commuting a life sentence might conclude, *See* Kimberly Metzer, "Resolving the 'False Dilemma': Simmons v. South Carolina and the Capital Sentencing Jury's Access to Parole Ineligibility Information," 27 U. Tol. Rev. 149, 167-73 (1995), that an error of judgment on its part would be corrected by another body of government.

9. Paraguay is not a "person" in Section 1983, *See* <u>Moor v. County of Alameda</u>, 411 U.S. 693, 699 (1973); <u>South Carolina v. Katzenbach</u>, 383 U.S. 301, 323-24 (1966), nor within a United States jurisdiction, either.

10. If the list that follows the colon makes up an integral part of the introductory sentence, writers should remember to indent all of each item and to number each item, to begin each item with a lower-case letter, to end each item except the last with a semicolon, to use a semicolon and "and" or "or" on the next-to-last item, and to conclude the last item with a period unless the list does not conclude the sentence.

◆ ◆ ◆ ◆

A lawyer is one who would trim
From the language all words that are slim;
To "he died after her"
He will always prefer
To aver that "she pre-deceased him."
—Laurence Perrine, Professor of English Emeritus, SMU, Dallas

◆ ◆ ◆ ◆

3

CHOOSING WORDS WITH STYLE

Precise word choice can mean the difference between success and failure. This chapter advises you to look, once again, at your draft to ensure that it says exactly what you intended.

OVERVIEW

◆ Jargon
◆ Wordiness
◆ Pronoun antecedents
◆ Noun strings
◆ Nominalizations
◆ Treacherous words
◆ Gender-based language

On a visit to St. Louis University School of Law, my husband and I were startled to see this sign on an elevator wall:

> FREE TED DREWS
>
> Thursday, Sept. 24
>
> Marchetti Office

Our concern for Mr. Drews' fate was overwhelmed by the laughter of students when we asked and were told that Ted Drews is St. Louis' famous ice cream; we were welcome to all we could eat.

Even common words can be treacherous if the reader is unaware of the local meaning!

◆ ◆ ◆ ◆

While engaged in the process of mutual and consensual romantic affections inside the vehicle, said vehicle engaged in a horizontal rollover, bringing injury to its occupants.

◆ ◆ ◆ ◆

JARGON

Every profession has its share of **jargon**, that specialized vocabulary used within a group with common backgrounds or interests. The use of jargon can save time—and imply an insider's connection. Newspapermen "put the issue to bed," and students sign up for classes on "M-W-F or T-T." This jargon is understood by everyone within that group but can baffle those outside it.

Terms of art, on the other hand, are a shorthand to underlying concepts. Attorneys depend on terms of art for daily communication among themselves: *dictum, garnishment, fee simple.* Readers untrained in the law cannot be expected to understand these terms, and, interestingly, many specialized words within one area of law confuse even other lawyers. For instance, car insurance policies can bewilder antitrust lawyers.

Legal writers inadvertently slip these specialized words and phrases into documents for laymen because they assume everyone else knows them also. Jargon, then, is a matter of **audience**. The needs of your audience must be met in each choice of word, just as they were met within your organizational choices.

SOLUTIONS

1. Identify and weed out **archaic legalisms**, i.e., words with plain English equivalents:

Archaic Legalism	Plain English
aforesaid	previous
forthwith	immediately
henceforth	from now on
herein	in this document
hereinafter	after this
thenceforth	after
thereafter	after that, accordingly
therein	in
theretofore	up to that time
hitherto	before
viz.	that is, *or* for example
whence	from what place, source
whereby	through, in accordance
said	the, that
whilst	during

2. Recognize **coupled synonyms**, which were useful hundreds of years ago when three languages (French, Latin, and versions of Old English) were used simultaneously on one English island, and replace them when practical[1] with one term your reader will understand:

---

[1] Be careful not to throw out necessary legal terms! For instance, "ready, willing, and able" are not legally redundant. Someone could be *willing* to share a document but not *ready* because the document has not been located. *See* TERRI LECLERCQ, *Jargon: Manure, Margarine, and Moderation*, EXPERT LEGAL WRITING 119, 122 (1995).

acknowledge and confess	act and deed
aid and abet	annul and set aside
authorize and empower	absolutely and completely
covenant and surmise	deem and consider
covenant and agree	each and every
due and payable	each and all
excess and unnecessary	false and untrue
final and conclusive	full and complete
fit and proper	have and hold
for and in consideration of	force and effect
fraud and deceit	in truth and in fact
in my stead and place	from and after
free and unfettered	let or hindrance
for and during	for and in consideration of
give, devise, and bequeath	keep and maintain
last will and testament	truth and veracity
lot, tract, or parcel of land	modified or changed
null, void, and of no effect	order and direct
ordered, judged, and decreed	save and except
type and kind	void and of no effect

3. **Eliminate** unnecessary, **overused** legal phrases that are a part of jargon and **replace** them with concrete references to a case name, the parties' names, and specific pronouns.

✗	in this instant case	in this case, here, [parties' names]
✗	the case at bar	this case
✗	one must prove	the plaintiff must prove
✗	the court below	the trial [district] court
✗	the said party	the plaintiff [defendant]

A major step in your growth as a law student is recognizing terms of art and working with them in both your thought process and your writing process. If you are given an Americans With Disabilities Act question, for example, you will work with statutory terms and apply your understanding of a certain term ("qualified individual" or "undue hardship") to the legislative-definition sections about the term, the case law, and perhaps legislative history for the term. Within all that help, you'll be the one to craft an understandable definition for your audience: your professor on an exam; the judge or your classmates; your client, who may or may not have a legal background.

TRY THESE

Find common terminology and shorter phrases to replace the following jargon.

1. TO THE HONORABLE JUDGE OF SAID COURT: NOW COME defendants in the above styled and numbered cause and file this their Motion for Directed Verdict, and request that the court direct the jury to return a verdict in this cause and in support would show as follows:

. . .

2. The prisoner was an exceptional *pro se* litigant relative to the many uneducated plaintiffs before the court.

3. Don Miller refutes this charge. The said party also contends that he has been unfairly enjoined into this suit.

4. She alleges violation of certain state law claims, to wit: fraud, breach of contract, and misrepresentation.

◆ ◆ ◆ ◆

Take the sentence, "The sky is blue." No junior associate would be so naive as to think this proposition could pass muster in a big firm. [H]e knows enough to say, "The sky is generally blue." [Or, f]or extra syllables, "The sky generally appears to be blue." A senior associate seeing this sentence [making corrections would say:] "In some parts of the world, what is generally thought of as the sky sometimes appears to be blue." DAN WHITE, *THE OFFICIAL LAWYER'S HANDBOOK* 177 (1983).

◆ ◆ ◆ ◆

WORDINESS

Legal documents frequently read as if the office copier has accidentally repeated a page, or as if the personal computer has mistakenly duplicated the previous paragraph.

Because repetition results in lengthy documents and uninteresting reading, focus on your drafts with a hungry eye. Imagine how much more forceful your prose will be if you **cut a fourth** from your draft.

SOLUTIONS

1. Omit unnecessary **prepositions**.

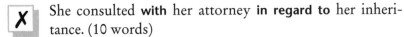 She consulted **with** her attorney **in regard to** her inheritance. (10 words)

She consulted her attorney **about** her inheritance. (7 words)

The **language of the statute** will not explicitly tell you what the legislature intended. (14 words)

The **statute's language** will not explicitly tell you the legislature's intention. (11 words)

2. Evaluate any **passive voice** verbs. (*See also* Chapter 2.)

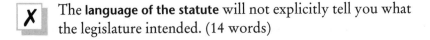 **It was held** by the court that the defendant was guilty of child abuse. (14 words)

The court held the defendant guilty of child abuse. (9 words)

3. Omit unnecessary **relative pronouns**.

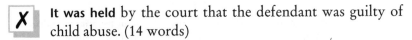 He was the man **who** knocked on your door. (9 words)

He knocked on your door. (5 words)

 He said **that** it was a problem **that** he would look into. (12 words)

He said he would look into the problem. (8 words)[2]

4. Omit **throat-clearers.**

✗ obviously	✗ clearly
✗ manifestly	✗ case is when
✗ as a matter of fact	✗ to tell the truth
✗ it is obvious that	✗ it is clear
✗ case is when	✗ situation is where
✗ it would appear to be the case that	

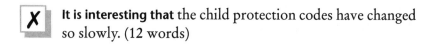

It is interesting that the child protection codes have changed so slowly. (12 words)

The child protection codes have changed slowly. (7 words)

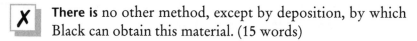

The **kind of** issue in these circumstances is probable cause. (10 words)

The issue in these circumstances is probable cause. (8 words)

5. Replace unnecessary **expletives,** e.g., "there is," "there are," and "it is."[3]

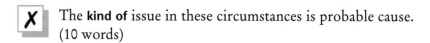

There is no other method, except by deposition, by which Black can obtain this material. (15 words)

Black cannot obtain this material except by deposition. (by words)

---

[2] There is no iron-clad rule about the inclusion of "that," so common sense will have to tell you when you have used too many, or when, because you've omitted the "that," you have lost the understanding that a relative pronoun provided.

[3] Some sentences may need to begin with "there is": "There is reason to worry today." It is clumsy and even wordier to revise this expletive into "A reason to worry today exists."

> **✗** **It is** important that fathers should continue to pay child support if the child chooses to attend college, even though the child is over the age of 18. (28 words)

Fathers should continue to pay child support if the child chooses to attend college, even though the child is over 18. (21 words)

6. Avoid **unnecessary modification** unless it serves a tactical purpose.

> **✗** The second defendant is plainly and unequivocally innocent. (8 words)

The second defendant is innocent. (5 words)

7. Watch for **redundancy**.

✗	alleged suspect	**✗**	irregardless (not a word)
✗	consensus of opinion	**✗**	next subsequent
✗	free gift	**✗**	personal (or honest) opinion
✗	rather (or most) unique	**✗**	single most
✗	the said party	**✗**	reason is becasue
✗	whether or not[4]		

> **✗** The **holdings** in <u>State v. Walker</u>, 441 S.W.2d 168 (Tex. 1969), and <u>State v. Schaffer</u>, 530 S.W.2d 813 (Tex. 1975), **hold** that new dissimilar construction bears doubtful relevance to the market value of condemned property.

---

[4] "Whether or not" is usually, but not always, redundant: *We do not know* **whether or not** *the executive summary will bring you immediate benefits (unnecessary "or not")*. But like most "rules," this one does not cover all possibilities: *Agency fees are collected to defray expenses of the activities of the union, expenses that benefit all members of the collective bargaining unit,* **whether union members or not**. Here the "or not" is syntactically necessary to complete the thought.

Which of these phrases and sentences can be shortened and yet not substantially changed?

1. for the purpose of evaluating

2. totally destroyed

3. went on to say that

4. mutual agreement

5. The obligation of the teacher may have existed in a moral way, but not in a legal way.

6. At a hearing on a request for a temporary injunction, the only question before the trial court is whether the applicant is entitled to preservation of the status quo of the subject matter of the suit pending a final trial of the case on the merits.

◆ ◆ ◆ ◆

"[L]awyers rely too heavily on forms without editing them. Because forms are written to cover every conceivable person and circumstance, by definition they are general, abstract, and sometimes even ambiguous. Because lawyers are usually not well-trained in English, they find it easier to copy a form than to edit it. The potential for lawsuits, however, including one for legal malpractice, makes it well worthwhile to make your documents as simple and as accessible to the reader as you can.
Susan Brody, et al., Legal Drafting 4 (1994)

◆ ◆ ◆ ◆

PRONOUN ANTECEDENTS

If a sentence containing a pronoun has more than one possible antecedent (noun) or if the antecedent is left unstated, then the reader is left wondering who did what with whom:

Detective Miller's counsel did not cross-examine Sharlot in the presence of the jury and now contends, as he did on direct appeal, that by not being able to go into Sharlot's background, **he** was prevented from showing his bias or prejudice for testifying as **he** did, in violation of **his** Sixth Amendment right to confrontation. [who is "he" and "him"?]

SOLUTIONS

1. Beware of **multiple antecedents.**[5]

X Because he was screaming abuses, the defendant ordered the police officer to arrest the man. [Who was screaming: The defendant? The police officer? The man? We need the pronoun attached to or replaced by one of the nouns for clarity.]

2. Be specific with **relative** and **demonstrative** pronouns.

Demonstrative pronouns	Relative pronouns
this	who, whom
that	that, which
these	what, whatever
	whomever, whoever
	whichever

X Under the scope of discovery in Rule 26(b)(3), "the court shall protect against disclosure of any mental impressions, conclusions, opinions, or legal theories of an attorney. . . ." **This** would seem to disallow interrogatory number two. [ambiguous demonstrative pronoun needs a concrete noun, e.g., "this rule," to follow it]

X "The actions of the merchant may impose liability, when reasonable questioning of the suspected shoplifter is not conducted," <u>Derouen v. Miller</u>, 614 So. 2d 1306 (La. Ct. App. 1993), **which** leads to the question whether the manager had the privilege to detain Jane Noel beyond one hour. [ambiguous reference: what leads?]

---

[5] Also see the Treacherous Placement section in Chapter 2.

X Bread for the World, a private, nonprofit organization, lobbies for national debt reduction for third-world countries **which** cannot pay for both needed food and government obligations to this country. [necessary clause (which cannot pay . . .) requires "that". See Punctuating Nonessentials, Chapter 4.]

TRY THESE

Rewrite the following sentences, replacing ambiguous pronouns and limiting the antecedent that a pronoun can refer to.

1. The question is whether Smith informed others of the defect in the computer board design and if this caused the loss of benefits Dell expected from these companies.

2. If there are cases on point with similar fact situations and you are discussing an issue that calls for argument, these will give more weight to your argument.

3. Thus, the "IV-D" plan requires that the State pursue reimbursement from absent parents for the public assistance provided for the necessary support of their children. The distribution of collections adheres to that.

♦ ♦ ♦ ♦

Cleansed of words without reason, much of the language
of the law need not be peculiar at all. And better for it.
DAVID MELLINKOFF, THE LANGUAGE OF THE LAW 454 (1963)

♦ ♦ ♦ ♦

NOUN STRINGS

Noun strings make legal writing dense and difficult. In a noun string, a succession of nouns modify each other; thus each preceding noun functions as an adjective that modifies the last noun:

The <u>bank's</u> <u>contract</u> <u>credit</u> <u>review</u> service
modifier   modifier   modifier modifier   noun

Until readers locate that final noun, they must assume that each noun **functions** as a noun, but after reading the whole string, they waste time and patience reprocessing those nouns into adjectives.

Noun strings camouflage the logical relationship between the nouns, and between the nouns and any adjective that may precede them.

 qualified scholarship funding bonds

- qualified-scholarship funding bonds?
- qualified scholarship-funding bonds?

 ten foot long concrete bars

- ten foot-long concrete bars
- ten-foot-long concrete bars

Solutions

1. Add a **hyphen** to connect two or more of the adjectives.

low-interest real estate loans
one-time tax write off

2. Unstring the noun string.

 a gross receipt sales tax

- a gross-receipt sales tax
- a sales tax on gross receipts

 new financial institutions franchises

- new financial-institutions franchises
- franchises for new financial institutions

Separate nouns and add connecting words or hyphens as necessary. Which terms are so ambiguous that the writer's intent cannot be determined?

1. certified return receipt amounts postcard receipt

2. funded welfare insurance programs

3. the bank's contract credit review service

◆ ◆ ◆ ◆

"The choice of exogenous variables in relation to multi-colinearity . . . is contingent upon the derivations of certain multiple correlation coefficients." . . . [This student's disease] attacks the best minds and gradually destroys the critical facilities, making it impossible for the sufferer to detect gibberish in his own writing or in that of others.
JAMES P. DEGNAN, "THE PH.D. ILLITERATE," THE WASHINGTON POST, Sept. 12, 1976 (quoted in RICHARD NEUMANN, JR., LEGAL REASONING AND LEGAL WRITING 138 (1994))

◆ ◆ ◆ ◆

NOMINALIZATIONS

Many a strong verb or concrete noun is hidden beneath a **nominalization**, those multisyllabic words with Latinate suffixes and prefixes such as -ize, -osity, -ate, -ability, -tion, -ancy, -ion, -al, -ence, -ive, -ment, de-, and mis- (examples: investiga**tion**, necess**itate**, intelli**gence**, **mis**appropriate). Although grammatically correct, nominalizations dilute a sentence by implying, rather than stating, the logical who/what relationships in the sentence.

 We made an **investigation** before we deposed the witness.

We **investigated** before deposing the witness.

 Despite the bank's **protestions**, the agency held it in contempt.

Although the bank **protested**, the agency held it in contempt.

SOLUTIONS

1. Watch for nouns created **from verbs:**

Nominalization	Verb Form
determination	to determine
resolution	to resolve
utilization	to use
reinforcement	to enforce
the addition of	to add
assumption	to assume
continuation	to continue

2. Also watch for nouns created from **adjectives** (that were once verbs):

Noun/Adjective	Original Verb
enforceability/enforceable	enforce
applicability/applicable	apply
specificity/specific	specify

 The formal consultive relationship will focus on the insights gained from current cost accounting and annuity depreciation for enhanced security performance measurement and evaluation.

We can measure and evaluate how the security performs.

A good check for your draft is to read each sentence separately, applying the "who did what to whom?" test.

TRY THESE

Identify any nominalizations, and rewrite to clarify the who/what action implied.

1. After thorough investigation of your deposition files, we advise that new coding is a necessary future addition.

2. Thank you for allowing our firm to make our presentation of international issues related to your business.

3. The consultant arrangement legitimates the transferability of testimony.

◆ ◆ ◆ ◆

I can assure you that reading this section will ensure your careful
word choice. I can't insure you for that knowledge, however.

◆ ◆ ◆ ◆

TREACHEROUS WORDS

A serious task for legal writers is choosing the exact and necessary word. Some words elude us as we draft; others sound correct in a context but aren't; some words are incorrect in any context. No one knows the meaning of every word or when to use each word he or she does know. But in legal writing, words are all you have, so it is essential to review the shades of difference between synonyms, for instance, and to keep track of those words you frequently misuse.

If you don't review your draft with a critical eye on word choice, you might provide unexpected repetition:

✗ The court's **holding** in <u>Katzenbach v. Morgan</u>, 384 U.S. 641 (1966), **held** that Section 4(e) of the 1965 Voting Rights Act was appropriate legislation to enforce the Equal Protection Clause.

71

Or you might create an oxymoron:

> **✗** The noise was a **continuous interruption** of his work. [Probably the writer meant "continual," occurring frequently, because a steady stream, occurring without interference, wouldn't be interrupting work as much as stopping any work.]

Or you might create a textual ambiguity:

> **✗** This is a key element in <u>Lopez</u> which distinguishes it from other Commerce Clause case law. [The writer may have intended to emphasize only the key element of <u>Lopez</u>, so she needed a comma after Lopez; or, the writer might have intended to point out that the key element distinguishes it from case law, and thus should have replaced the "which" with "that" to signal an essential and necessary clause.]

Readers can also jump to the conclusion that a legal writer isn't particularly educated (or awake) if many word errors blot a document.

SOLUTIONS

1. Consult **professional sources** like Wilson Follett, *Modern American Usage: A Guide*; W.H. Fowler, *A Dictionary of Modern English Usage*; David Mellinkoff, *Mellinkoff's Dictionary of American Legal Usage* (1990). From them, **study** those words frequently misused.

allusion/illusion	historic/historical
anxious/eager	i.e., e.g.
as/because	imply/infer
as/when	moot
assume/presume	oral/verbal
bimonthly/semimonthly	prescribe/proscribe
clearly	respectively
credible/credulous	that/which
different than	that/who

2. Create **your own list** of words that confuse you or that you frequently misuse. Keep the list in your computer thesaurus or on a list near your writing area.

TRY THESE

Investigate the word choice in these examples. Eliminate repetitions and oxymorons, and edit for ambiguous or misused words.

1. Nothing in this case warrants applying for a different standard than that in <u>Estelle v. Gamble</u>.

2. As the clerk turned back to face his customer, he noticed the necklace and customer were gone.

3. Dr. Jones suggested that Mrs. Baker hire someone to monitor her work and insure that medicine was properly charted.

4. The therapist posited various possible cases for the child's anxiety, i.e., travel between two households, parental inability to communicate, incorporation into contrasting religious activities, and concern for both parents, etc.

◆ ◆ ◆ ◆

An attorney worried all morning over the awkward options for beginning a letter to one female and four male bankers. Rather than the bulky "Dear Sirs and Madam," his solution was to drop the woman's name from the inside address list, address the letter "Dear Sirs," and add at the bottom of the letter, "c.c. Texanna McPhail."

◆ ◆ ◆ ◆

GENDER-BASED LANGUAGE

Historically, the English language used masculine **nouns** as generic placeholders for both genders (<u>mankind</u>, <u>fireman</u>). Similarly, English has a tradition that gender-based **pronouns** reflect both genders. (An attorney should call <u>his</u> office.) Today, however, linguists and psychologists have made us aware of the subliminal impact that this historical tradition has had on our society,[6] and the law's role in the perpetuation of that impact.

Perhaps, someday, someone will invent a new third-person pronoun with no gender implications. Right now, though, legal stylists can avoid limiting society to its masculine components through the following alternatives.

SOLUTIONS

1. Switch your sentence to the **third person plural** where possible:

 Everyone is expected to take his clients to lunch.

All attorneys are expected to take their clients to lunch.

The partners expect all third-year associates to take their clients to lunch.

Don't make this change if the result creates ambiguity:

 Each of the associates decided their Friday wardrobes should be casual. ("Each" is a singular noun requiring a singular pronoun.)

All of the associates decided their Friday wardrobes should be casual.

Each of the associates decided his or her Friday wardrobe should be casual.

---

[6] See, for instance, a thorough discussion of both the historical justifications for using the masculine pronoun as "pseudogeneric" and a summary of psychological studies about its impact, in DEBORA SCHEIKART, "The Gender Neutral Pronoun Redefined," 20 WOMEN'S RIGHTS L. REPORTER, 1.

2. Drop the pronoun where possible:

 The average prisoner calls his lawyer in the first hour of his arrest.

The average prisoner calls a lawyer in the first hour of arrest.

3. Refer to people by **occupation or qualification** instead of gender.

 Improvement in water quality in major cities is man's goal for the next decade.

The voters' goal for the next decade is improvement in water quality in major cities.

4. Vary the document's pronouns from "he" to "she"—if and only if the variation does not change the meaning of your document and does not result in utter silliness.

 Many practicing attorneys dream of becoming law professors. One may want to leave his 60-hour week behind. She may look forward to the intellectual stimulation of her imagined students.

TRY THESE

What would you do about word choice in the following situations?

1. You are returning a business letter to a banker, who has signed an initial inquiry as "J.W. Smith." What is a proper salutation?

2. Preparing a group-mailing tax advice letter to a group of sculptors, you need to refer to the artist who has traveling exhibitions, to the artist who uses a publicist, etc. How do you avoid the "he" or "she" pronoun?

3. As you prepare a brief for your client, you realize that she is an ardent feminist and that you have consistently used "he" as a generic reference to "anyone under the law who . . . ." Now what?

75

WHAT TO REMEMBER

Responsibility for clear and concise language rests with you. Only by examining a contract or memorandum word for word, while considering each idea in relation to surrounding ideas, can you anticipate any ensuing confusion. That's your role both as a student writer now and as a practicing attorney later: to satisfy the current needs of the drafters and the future needs of all possible audiences. You can nurture and develop your ability through a lifelong investigation of words; the study of legal precedent and scholarship; and especially the study of style in news magazines, advertisements, political essays, and even novels.

CONCLUDING EXERCISES

Grade yourself on correcting these concluding quizzes that mix the word problems you've just reviewed. You'll find possible answers in the Appendix.

Word Quiz 1

1. It is well established that the design of roads and bridges is a discretionary function, and the State will not be liable for such decisions, which is consistent with cases that hold decisions made at the policy level instead of operational level are immune.
2. The lack of attendance has created the situation where we do not know the status of work items. Therefore, we cannot access our ability to accomplish the schedule.
3. Thank you for your anticipated assistance promoting resolution to these issues.

4. parent company debt service requirements
5. Each member of the law school community must report to the Associate Dean any conduct he or she has reason to believe violated the Rules of Professional Conduct which raises a question as to the honesty, trustworthiness, or fitness of the student to become a lawyer.
6. Please attend to the organization of the current files concerning the deposition of V. Miles.
7. six inch thick concrete pallets
8. The sales price would have been taxable whether or not the book was sold directly to the vendors or to the end consumer.
9. When a pilot arrives in the cockpit, he needs to review all current logs and check his gauges before takeoff.
10. The labor law course has as it's goal the delineation of workers and bosses.

Word Quiz 2

1. The definition provided by the statute must be applied in order to prove that a person is guilty.
2. The municipality would have the information concerning the location of the arrest and the identity of the co-defendant policeman in its possession, and the defendant could easily combine this information with the information contained in the complaint. It will probably provide a sufficiently specific factual basis for the time of the alleged violation, the place where it occurred, and those responsible.
3. well established common law cause of action
4. This effort was made in a most callous way.
5. the correct substantive evidence rule test
6. The Commission's revisions of its rules comprehensively addressed the question of beneficial ownership.
7. It is important to note that the earlier discussion of the computation of time periods is relevant here . . . . However, it must be noted that under one statutory interpretation, the ninety-day period is computed from the original due date.

8. The court in <u>Matthews</u> held that where "plain, adequate, and complete" relief is available, the aggrieved party "is left to that remedy in the state courts" unless a federal question is involved. 284 U.S. 526 (1927). Following the enactment of § 1341 in 1937, this theme was broadened by the U.S. Supreme Court.

9. It can not be said that the plaintiff created a passive web site.

10. When a medical expert gives evidence throughout the trial, he must weigh the seriousness of the injury against both his medical expertise and his professional experience.

Punctuation has long been considered the stronghold of inflexible
and prescriptive rules. This tradition is unfortunate. To a great degree,
punctuation is variable, flexible, and even imaginative.
William D. Drake, The Way to Punctuate, XII (1971).

"[I]n old manuscripts, words were not even separated until the 8th
century A.D. . . . the comma as we know and use with casual indifference,
and occasionally for stunning efficacy, is seen as a relatively
modern device for presenting a visual equivalent of that rise and fall
of speech and rational discourse."
Jack Matthews, "The Philosophy of The Comma,"
Soundings Summer/Fall 1997, 435

4

PUNCTUATING WITH STYLE

This is your last look at your draft: This time, return to that organized, polished document you're creating, and review the punctuation that holds it together, separates portions of it, and advises your readers about both its pace and meaning.

OVERVIEW

- General punctuation rules
- Additional legal-writing punctuation rules
- Punctuation as roadsigns for readers

[Answer is located ▶
at end of chapter.]

Who has more than one brother, and how did you know?

A. Daniel Keller and his brother Kenneth Keller have owned the station for five years.

B. Daniel Miller and his brother, Kenneth Miller, have owned the station for five years.

When early writers added punctuation to their written speeches in the third century B.C., they signaled places for speakers to pause. The different marks signaled the length of pause for the reader/speaker. Today's punctuation is governed by only a few rules for those signals.

GENERAL PUNCTUATION RULES

Notice where periods and commas are placed in the first sentence patterns below:

1. Complete sentence.

2. Complete sentence; complete sentence.

3. Complete sentence ; therefore, complete sentence.
; however,
; nevertheless,
; consequently
; furthermore,

4. Complete   ,   on the other hand,   sentence.
                        ,   for example,
                        ,   in fact,

5. Although   incomplete sentence,   complete sentence.
      After
      Because
      While
      When

6. Complete sentence   although   incomplete sentence.
                            after
                            because
                            while
                            when

7. Sentence ending: list or dramatic saying follows colon.

8. Commas and periods, like "these," go inside quotation marks.

Ghandi said, "People do not need to be governed—only the top five percent who are avarous and hoarders, and the bottom five percent who are common thieves and murderers need governing."

Ghandi, who said "[p]eople do not need to be governed—only the top five percent who are avarous and hoarders, and the bottom five percent who are common thieves and murderers need governing," will always be my hero.

9. Colons and semicolons go "outside"; this rule is an American rule.

He testified that he "wanted to play by the rules"; unfortunately, he did not know this society's rules.

Counsel protested the court's understanding of "genuine issue": whether a reasonable jury could resolve the fact for one side or the other.

ADDITIONAL RULES FOR LEGAL WRITERS

Technical writing adds additional rules to help writers achieve precision.

10. Complete sentence   , and   complete sentence.
, or
, nor
, but
, yet

The comma is not always essential in all types of writing, but legal writers signal an impending new subject/verb with it.

 The plaintiff's car hit the newsstand and the driver behind him failed to stop.

11. Sentence contains an item, item, and item.
Sentence contains an item; another item, with its own comma; and another item will require semicolons.

He was accused of breaking and entering, assault and battery, and rape.

Protesters against the School of the Americas came to Ft. Benning, Georgia, from as far away as Austin, Texas; Boca Raton, Florida; Danbury, Connecticut; Mexico; El Salvador; and many European countries.

12. Textual citations require a set of commas.

The "minimum contacts" framework, in <u>Mellon Bank v. Farrino</u>, 960 F.2d 1217, 1221 (3rd Cir. 1992), followed that announced in <u>International Shoe</u>.

13. Ellipses and spacing indicate that you have omitted material from a passage being quoted. (A legal ellipsis mark is composed of **three spaced** periods.)

When you omit material **after** a period in the text, you add a fourth dot to include the final punctuation mark; the first dot is the period, so you type no space between it and the preceding word if the original text includes a period. If you omit material **before** that sentence ends, then follow it with a space before the first dot.[1] You should have a complete sentence on both sides of the four-dot ellipsis.

Students worry about final examinations from their first week in classes. They should take the advice of Charles Calleros:

Most essay examinations ask for a balanced analysis of a problem with a direction . . . . Like an actual office memorandum assignment, the exam problem may identify one of the parties as your client. . . . [Y]ou must anticipate and demonstrate an understanding of the counterarguments that the opposing party likely will raise.

. . .

[a]n answer to an essay examination and the discussion section of an office memorandum typically share a general structure: After (1) identifying the issue, you should (2) summarize the applicable legal rule or rules, (3) apply the rule to the relevant facts to determine whether the facts satisfy the rule, and (4) state a reasonable conclusion.

Charles Calleros, *Legal Method and Writing 137 (1994)*

Legal writers do not use ellipsis points before a block quotation beginning with a complete sentence even though they have (usually) left out material from the original.

14. Brackets signal change in quoted material:[2]
   (a) missing words or letters;
   (b) capitals changed to lower case and lower-cased words changed to capitals to fit the sense of the quotation into your text;
   (c) additions that help explain ambiguous material in a quotation;

---

[1] THE BLUEBOOK: A UNIFORM SYSTEM OF CITATION, Rule 5.3(b)(ii) (16th ed. 1996).
[2] THE BLUEBOOK: A UNIFORM SYSTEM OF CITATION, Rule 5.2 (16th ed. 1996).

83

> (d) your own comments inserted into quoted material; and
> (e) the word "sic" to indicate an error repeated from the original ("sic" is a complete word meaning "in this manner" or "thus").

Following are examples of correctly placed brackets:

Mark Wojcik suggested, "The book [*Introduction to Legal English*] can and should be supplemented with additional materials."

The contract specifically provides that "$10,000 shall be paid to the surrogate [appellant] upon entry of the judgment fully terminating parental rights of the surrogate." See Surrogate Mother Contract Agreement § 4.

"[P]risoner petitions . . . are the first line of defence against unconstitutional violations." Bounds v. Smith, 430 U.S. 817, 827, 97 S. Ct. 1491, 1498 (1977).

The letter thanked me for "speaking to the State Bar and exposing [sic]" myself to that many lawyers.

Other than those rules, most punctuation is optional. Your choice of punctuation announces to your reader the number and length of pauses you want them to take. First you have to decide what message you want to send your readers.

PUNCTUATION AS ROADSIGNS

I. To make readers STOP completely for a moment:

Use a Period

Periods generally signal the conclusion of a complete, independent clause, like this one. (Or incomplete, if you desire informality.)

II. To make readers **STOP BUT IMMEDIATELY READ ON**:

A. Use a Semicolon

Semicolons signal a pause weaker than a period but stronger than a comma; notice that it contains both a period ("stop") and a comma ("pause but go").

> By the plain language of Rule 68, only the terms of the judgment finally obtained may be compared to the offer of judgment; non-judgment relief is not included.

B. Use a Comma with a Subsequent Conjunction

When coupled immediately with a conjunction, a comma invites a quick continuation despite the shift in subject.

> The law school required a personal statement, but the applicant decided he had nothing personal to say.

C. Use a Colon

A colon signals a pause stronger that a semicolon and suggests a more direct relationship between two ideas: it tells the reader that what follows will illustrate or amplify what has gone before.

> Ghandi admitted to authorities that he knew a lot about prisons: African and Indian.

III. To ask readers to **PAUSE**, to **SLOW DOWN** for a short moment:

A. Use a Comma

1. Writers need a comma after an introductory clause with its own subject and verb to warn readers that the main subject and verb are next.

Because I could not stop for Death, He kindly stopped for me.

2. Writers have an option of slowing readers down after a short introductory clause or phrase.

By July 1990 he had turned in his resignation.
By July 1990, he had turned in his resignation.

Inadequate punctuation of some short introductory phrases, however, can confuse readers. See if you can process this sentence the first time you read it:

 In each one word is missing.

In each, one word is missing.

3. Similarly, legal writers can signal nonessential (parenthetical) or explanatory information with a pair of commas.

It is up to Congress, not the courts, to change the law.

The new secretary, however good she may be, will have to be replaced by someone with seniority.

The commas mark the boundaries of the interrupting phrase or clause, so use *two commas* unless one is replaced by some other punctuation mark. (It is easy to remember to use two commas if you compare them to parentheses.)

If your explanation limits, restricts, or defines the modified word, it is functioning as a restrictive phrase that answers the question "which one?" and thus narrows the sentence to that subcategory. A restrictive phrase is *not* set off with commas.

Tomorrow you can use the car that is in the garage. (there are other cars around)

On the other hand, if your explanatory information does not restrict the meaning but is instead merely useful, relegate it to a subordinate position through the use of commas.

Tomorrow you can drive my car, which is in the garage. (only car)

A nonrestrictive phrase or clause describes, or gives additional information, about the *entire* category that has already been named.

The backpacks, **which** are made in offshore sweatshops, are labeled "Made in the U.S.A." (All of this group of backpacks are labeled—their background is not essential to narrow the group.)

The backpacks **that** are made in off-shore sweatshops are labeled "Made in the U.S.A." (Of many different backpacks from different sources, these backpacks [limited group] came from off-shore sweatshops.)

IV. To **OFFER A LIST**:

When the list is a grammatical part of the sentence, the items to be enumerated must belong to the same class, with a common idea introduced before the colon. Then, for lists within a formal text, writers can choose to set the list apart from the text by:

1. introducing the list with a colon;
2. indenting all of each item and numbering each item;
3. beginning each item with a lower-case letter;
4. concluding each item but the last with a semicolon;
5. placing a semicolon and "and" or "or" after the next-to-last item; and
6. concluding the item with a period unless the list does not conclude the textual sentence.

If writers choose to create a list that follows a complete sentence but is **not** a part of the textual sentence's grammar, then they must switch capitalization and punctuation conventions to match. Writers should follow the following seven conventions:

1. Colon introduction.
2. Indentation.
3. Grammatical parallel.
4. Capital letters.
5. Numbered items.
6. Periods at the end of each item.
7. No "or" or "and" for culmination.

If you have created a long list of textual phrases, semicolons can help readers follow your hierarchy:

Law schools need applicants who do not choose their schools based merely on rankings; who do not abuse classmates to get the attention of professors; who enter their first year to learn and not just to make an A; who are not afraid of risk; whose ambitions are big enough to include others; who know how to balance their lives with exercise and sleep and family; whose commitment to the world beyond them takes them into a world that needs them; who enter the profession to uplift it in the public esteem; who do not believe that competition, and "Ramboism," and knowing the boss are the three keys to success. In short, the law schools need applicants who will be moral leaders.

If legal writers create an informal document or want to highlight a series of items that are not necessarily grammatically parallel, they can use bullet dots and other typographical cues instead of numbers.

V. To PULL WORDS TOGETHER so readers recognize a thought unit:

Use a Hyphen

1. When writers choose to combine two adjectives into one descriptive adjective before a noun, they combine the adjectives with a hyphen:

 The state sponsored negotiators offered a week of free negotiations to help clear the courts' dockets.

This string of words before the noun functions as a compound adjective and needs to be hyphenated: the state-sponsored negotiations. The hyphen creates a bond between the two words so that they can correctly be read as a compound adjective before the main noun "negotiators." Remember, however, that adverbs ending in -ly cannot be hyphenated. (*See* Chapter 3.)

2. If two nouns function as adjectives before a chosen noun, writers generally choose to hyphenate them to aid clarity (see Chapter 3):

 the remedy and repair limitation provision

the remedy- and repair-limitation provision

Once hyphenated, the noun-adjective units are broken from the string. A second option to clarify noun strings is to relocate portions of them away from the string:

the provision that limits remedy and repair

VI. To **PUSH WORDS APART** from the text so readers recognize the need for a long pause:

A. Use a Dash

Dashes signal a break in thought and writing—and thus legal writers are more reluctant to use them than, for instance, novelists are. But dashes have their place in any writing. Dashes can function like a colon, indicating something will follow an independent clause. Therefore, if the connection is obvious and you want to emphasize that a classifying clause follows, the dash remains a cautious option:

> Over $1.4 billion per year of new juvenile detention facilities and prisons are not stanching the growing alienation and violence among our young, who lack a purposeful, joyful song to sing in life—a song that is learned first in the home and reinforced in school and in other community institutions and by the religious and political values and climate in our society.
>
> Marian Wright Edelman
> *53 The Measure of Our Successs (1994)*

The court has one consistent goal--to provide justice for the people of this state.

Dashes differ from hyphens in both typography and purpose. Dashes are typed with two hyphens and no spaces on either side. Dashes *separate*; hyphens draw together.

The red-hot issue this semester was faculty diversity.

Faculty diversity was an issue across the campus this semester--a hot issue.

B. Use a Colon

Colons signal that material promised or suggested will follow; thus, quotations, questions, explanations, and enumerations follow a colon.

Our law firm has only two rules: (1) research, research, research, and (2) the boss is always right.

Colons are used to introduce material that is not a normal part of the sentence's grammar. Writers should not use them between a verb and its complement or object, between a preposition and its object, or after "such as" and "including" unless the material to follow is tabulated on separate lines.

 A prisoner has: no privacy of mail and little access to medical treatment.

 The law firm sent a request that he send his resume including: educational background, work experience, and references.

Capitalization after a colon is optional, but most writers capitalize complete sentences after the colon and leave fragments in lower case:

We must all accept a priority: Your priority was never on my list.

The student went to law school for personal reasons: his bank account and his parents.

VII. To signal a **DIRECT QUOTATION** or signal readers that **A WORD IS USED AS A WORD**:

Legal writers frequently have the option of paraphrasing ideas or of using direct quotations with precedent, but once the decision is made to quote someone's actual words, then quotation marks are required.

A. Use Quotation Marks

1. You must use quotation marks when you quote a word or phrase within your text:

The attorney was worried about the "chilling effect of the undocumented evidence." (Cite.)

2. If the quotation is longer than 49 words (or if you have a special reason for setting quoted material outside your main text),[3] signal the indented quotation with single-spaced indented format but do *not* use quotation marks: the formatting signals the direct quotation. If the quotation is not a part of your textual sentence, lead into it with a colon. If the quotation picks up your textual syntax, do not add any punctuation before indenting and single spacing.

The number of judges cannot keep up with the demands of society. We need more judges:

> For example, in less than two decades, the total number of filings in California has increased 176% in the Supreme Court and 438% in the courts of appeal, yet there has been no like increase in the number of judges.

The number of judges cannot keep up with the demands of society. According to S. Eric Ottesen, we need more judges because in less than twenty years

> the total number of filings in California has increased 176% in the Supreme Court and 438% in the courts of appeal, yet there has been no like increase in the number of judges.

Unlike the conventions of other writing styles, however, legal writers must follow the BLUEBOOK rule to maintain the original quotation marks within a quotation.[4]

3. You can use quotation marks to highlight that a word is intended to mean something different from its original definition or indicate a word you will define:

---

[3] THE BLUEBOOK: A UNIFORM SYSTEM OF CITATION, Rule 5.1 (16th ed. 1996).
[4] THE BLUEBOOK: A UNIFORM SYSTEM OF CITATION, Rule 5.1(a) (16th ed. 1996).

His idea of a "great time" was to review last week's cases.

By "successful student," the law school means someone with grades good enough for law review.

Italics may be used here, also: His definition of a *good time* was to review last week's cases. By *successful student*, the law school means someone with grades good enough for law review.

VIII. To distinguish between and **POSSESSIVE AND PLURALS**, learn to use apostrophes correctly:

A. Possessives Take Apostrophes

English nouns require apostrophes to signal possession.

> Student's notebook (one student)
> Students' notebooks (more than one student and notebook)

English pronouns have their own possessive case (his, my, their, our) and **do not** require an apostrophe.

 The company determined it's future with a quick vote.

B. Plurals Do Not Require an Apostrophe

Writing specialists disagree about the use of an apostrophe to make a number, date, proper noun, or letter plural. The BLUEBOOK is silent on this problem, so the best advice is to be consistent to one authority, like *The Chicago Manual of Style*, which recommends not using apostrophes in these plurals.[5]

---

[5] THE CHICAGO MANUAL OF STYLE, UNIVERSITY OF CHICAGO PRESS 8.64 (1993).

All winners of the 1000s were given ten one-hundred dollar bills.

 The Miller's were visiting their daughter when the car crashed through the wall.

The 60s were a period of protest and freedom.

 The professor awarded only three TA's a job offer.

The professor awarded only three TAs a job offer.

WHAT TO REMEMBER

As boring as punctuation rules may seem, they nevertheless perform an important role in communicating. English doesn't have so many punctuation rules that they overwhelm writers, so learn the few rules; study the options; then allow yourself some play—readers will appreciate it and see your educated variances as a sign of intelligence.

Answer to ▶
Question, p. 00

A. Daniel Keller has more than one brother; placing no commas around "Kenneth Keller" signals that his name is necessary to delineate him from other brothers.

B. Daniel Miller has only one; the commas act as a parenthesis, making Kenneth's name unnecessary because he is the only brother.

CONCLUDING EXERCISES

Grade yourself on correcting these concluding quizzes that mix the punctuation rules you have just reviewed. (You'll find possible answers in the Appendix.)

Punctuation Quiz 1

1. However, to be granted judicial relief for misappropriation of a trade secret the plaintiff must prove by a preponderance of the evidence the following elements.
2. The suit should have been brought against M.B. Beazly, Administrator of the estate, Mike Koby, the attorney for the estate, and Jim Mattox, the Attorney General.
3. The issue of the insolvency of a debtor is a question of fact and solvency may be determined proximately before or immediately after the time of the transfer.
4. Not many graduates are without major debts certainly we can list none from our section.
5. The common law doctrine of negligence consists of three essential elements—a legal duty owed by one person to another, a breach of that duty, and damages proximately caused by that breach.
6. Course and scope of employment is defined in Section 101.001(B)(4) as:

   . . . the performance for a governmental unit of the duties of an employee's office of employment and includes being in or about the performance of tasks lawfully assigned to an employee by competent authority.

7. The attorney returned her fee which was under dispute.
8. Mr. Marshall also claims that during the arrest Officer Breeger became "highly abusive", denied Mr. Marshall his right to speak and struck the plaintiff twice, without provocation, causing him bodily injury.
9. In the decision in <u>Santex,</u> supra, the court also held that the employee need prove only that filing the claim was a reason for termination not the sole reason.
10. Plaintiff further argued that the statute did not apply because the unit was only a component part of a larger whole; thus not, by itself, an "improvement."

Punctuation Quiz 2

1. Such participation, he claims was fundamentally unfair.
2. The audit was correct, because the seven customer contracts stated material and equipment, labor, and sales tax as separated amounts.
3. The second issue of first impression is whether the reservation of the power to prosecute, compromise and settle or otherwise deal with any claim for additional royalties is illegal and void any attempt to engage in the unauthorized practice of law.
4. Each of the Constitution's Amendments has the same purpose each protects us from ourselves.
5. A statement apparently made to the EEOC by Weeks shows that Weeks spends only 50% of his time developing new business; whereas, Johnson spent all of his time developing new business.
6. This Court, in <u>Benson v. McMahon</u>, 127 U.S. 457,463 (1888) has equated this showing to that required for a preliminary hearing in domestic arrest situations.
7. The defendant hoped to ignore the notice -- pretend she did not receive it.
8. The company sent twelve 1040's on the same day.
9. In re Extradition of Russell, the Court of Appeals for the Fifth Circuit echoed the Second Circuit's reasoning:

   . . . the 'information' was allowed to be informal in character, as opposed to substance . . . the provisional arrest request . . . could be made directly between the Justice ministries . . .

10. In the first class students were called on alphabetically.

5

FORMATTING FOR A VISUAL SOCIETY

Remember the advice in the Preface: Your readers are not going to look at your document because they have extra time or because they need entertainment. Rather, they need information—and fast. To help them find that information, writers should make each document as attractive and accessible as possible. You are already the victim of the subliminal seduction of law schools: All opinions look like each other, and all sample memoranda look like other sample memoranda. You need to remember your own dismay at your first sight of these documents and break the pattern by making pages that are

- visually inviting,
- logically organized, and
- understandable on the first reading.

OVERVIEW

- ◆ Student memorandum with and without white space and headings
- ◆ Client letter with and without white space and tabulation
- ◆ Judicial opinion with and without white space, headings, and initial road map
- ◆ Sexual harassment policy with and without white space, headings, and graphics
- ◆ Sample paragraphs with and without sentence length variety, capital letters, and tabulation

SOLUTIONS:

1. Add **white space** throughout the document with margin, spaces between paragraphs, space around tabulation, graphics.

2. Create an **initial road map** that contains both the conclusion and brief roadmap of what will follow.

3. Adjust **paragraphs' lengths** so that they are not all the same (long) length.

4. For client documents, include **side bars** for summaries or headings.

5. Include **graphics** where possible, and label them so readers can skim the accompanying text.

6. **Avoid ALL CAPITAL LETTERS** where possible (don't change trademark names, or capital/strikeout system of some legislation).

7. Place explanatory material and history in an **appendix** at the end of a document.

Example 1. A sample student memorandum

QUESTION PRESENTED: Does an actor satisfy the intent element of a battery claim when she causes an unintended harm to an unintended victim?

CONCLUSION: Yes. First, the intent element of a battery action is satisfied against an actor who causes an unintended harm to an unintended victim. Also, if an actor intended to cause a particular harm, her intent in that regard can be transferred to the harm actually resulting from her action. Specific intent is not required with regard to the harm caused or the recipient of the harm. . . .

FACTS: Lima surprised two apparent thieves in prize-winning peach trees. She ran at them, shouting, and fired two warning shots above and to the right of them. Gerardi heard the first shot and saw the trespassers fleeing Lima's property. The second shot struck Gerardi in the leg. Gerardi has threatened to sue Lima for battery, claiming damages. . . .

DISCUSSION: Gerardi's battery claim against Lima hinges on the legal issue of the transferability of Lima's intent in causing the harm inflicted upon Gerardi. Intent to cause a harm is not limited to the intended recipient of the harm. Specific intent with regard to the particular recipient of the injury is not required in a tort action for assault and battery. Morrow v. Flores, 225 S.W.2d 621, 623-24 (Tex. Civ. App.—Fort Worth 1949, writ ref'd n.r.e.). Also, intent to cause a harm in a tort action is not limited to the actor's intended harm. . . .

Requisite intent is an essential element of a battery action. There are two rules of law regarding intent relevant to this case. The first rule of law is concerned with the actor's intent in causing a harm to a person different from the person intended to receive the harm. . . .

This counter argument ignores the nature of the transfers of intent and the policy considerations behind the holdings of Bennight and Morrow. . . . It would be inconsistent with these policy goals to have a situation where liability would be reduced in a situation where a person acted so irresponsibly that she caused an unintended harm to an unintended recipient. A combination of the holdings of Bennight and Morrow is consistent with their policy goals and is appropriate.

Example 1B. Student memorandum with headings,
white space, and initial road map

QUESTION PRESENTED: Does an actor satisfy the intent element of a battery claim when she causes an unintended harm to an unintended victim?

CONCLUSION: Yes. **First**, the intent element of a battery action is satisfied against an actor who causes an unintended harm to an unintended victim. **Second**, if an actor intended to cause a particular harm, her intent can be transferred to the harm actually resulting from her action. . . .

FACTS: Lima surprised two apparent thieves in prize-winning peach trees. She ran at them, shouting, and fired two warning shots above and to the right of them. Gerardi heard the first shot and saw the trespassers fleeing Lima's property. The second shot struck Gerardi in the leg. Gerardi has threatened to sue Lima for battery, claiming damages. . . .

DISCUSSION: Lima satisfies the intent element of a battery claim when she caused an unintended harm to Gerardi, an unintended victim. Gerardi's battery claim against Lima hinges on the legal issue of the transferability of Lima's intent in causing the harm inflicted upon Gerardi. **First**, intent to cause a harm is not limited to the intended recipient of the harm. . . .

Intent to Case the Harm to Unintended Victim

Requisite intent is an essential element of a battery action. There are two rules of law regarding intent relevant to this case. The first rule of law is concerned with the actor's intent in causing a harm to a person different from the person intended to receive the harm. . . .

Conclusion Applying Policy

This double-transfer counter argument ignores the nature of the transfers of intent and the policy considerations behind the holdings of <u>Bennight</u> and <u>Morrow</u>. . . .

A combination of the holdings of <u>Bennight</u> and <u>Morrow</u> is consistent with their policy goals and is appropriate. The intent element of a battery claim against Lima should be satisfied.

101

Example 2A. Client letter emphasizing content only

GETMAN & SELCOV, LLP   ATTORNEYS AT LAW

52 S. Manheim Blvd., 2nd Floor   (914) 255-9370
New Paltz, NY 12561   fax (914) 255-3629

Julius Getman (DC bar only), of counsel   Richard B. Wolf (NY and DC), of counsel

April 5, 2000

VIA FEDERAL EXPRESS

Professor David Sokolow
University of Texas Law School
727 E. 26th Street
Austin, Texas 78702

Dear Professor Sokolow:

Please find enclosed a Subpoena Duces Tecum Without Deposition which has been issued by the U.S. District Court, Middle District of Florida, Jacksonville Division, Case No. 99-978-Civ-J-11D, for any and all documents regarding Toby Billings (DOB: 9/16/46; SSN: 458-48-3195). We would appreciate your providing any and all items in the attached subpoena. These documents should include a complete statement of all opinions expressed and the basis and reasons therefor; the data or other information considered in forming the opinion(s); any exhibits to be used as a summary of or support for the opinion(s); expert qualifications, including a list of all publications authored within the preceding ten years (include your resume); compensation amount(s); and a list of cases in which you have testified as an expert at trial or by deposition within the preceding four years.

Please submit your statement for reproduction charges, and we will reimburse you that same amount. Thank you for your assistance in this matter. Please do not hesitate to call if you require further information.

Yours truly,

Susan Sharlot
Legal Assistant

Example 2B. Revised client letter: white space, tabulation, bold face

---

GETMAN & SELCOV, LLP   ATTORNEYS AT LAW

52 S. Manheim Blvd., 2nd Floor   (914) 255-9370
New Paltz, NY 12561   fax (914) 255-3629

Julius Getman (DC bar only), of counsel   Richard B. Wolf (NY and DC), of counsel

July 5, 2000

VIA FEDERAL EXPRESS

Professor David Sokolow
University of Texas Law School
727 E. 26th Street
Austin, Texas 78702

RE: Toby Billings vs. Immortal Faces
Case No. 99-978-Civ-J-11D

Dear Professor Sokolow:

We are asking that you comply with the Subpoena Duces Tecum Without Deposition in this case. The U.S. District Court, Middle District of Florida, Jacksonville Division, asks for any and all documents regarding Toby Billings (DOB: 9/16/46; SSN: 458-48-3195). We would appreciate your providing any items in the attached subpoena, including:

1. a complete statement of all **opinions** expressed and the basis and **reasons** therefor;
2. the **data or other information** considered in forming the opinion(s);
3. any **exhibits** to be used as a summary of or support for the opinion(s);
4. **expert qualifications,** including a list of all publications authored within the preceding ten years (include your resume);
5. **compensation** amount(s); and
6. a **list of cases** in which you have testified as an expert at trial or by deposition within the preceding four years.

As you will see, the **deadline** for this information in **May 5, 2000.**

If you will submit your statement for reproduction charges, we will reimburse you that same amount. Thank you for assisting us. Please do not hesitate to call me if you require further information.

Yours truly,

Susan Sharlot
Legal Assistant

Example 3A. 1965 D.C. Court of Appeals Opinion

Ora Lee WILLIAMS,
Appellant
v.
WALKER-THOMAS
FURNITURE
COMPANY, Appellee,

William THORNE
et al., Appellants,
v.
WALKER-THOMAS
FURNITURE
COMPANY, Appellee.
Nos. 18604, 18605.

United States Court
of Appeals
District of Columbia
Circuit.

Argued April 9, 1965.
Decided Aug. 11, 1965.

J. SKELLY WRIGHT, Circuit Judge:

Appellee, Walker-Thomas Furniture Company, operates a retail furniture store in the District of Columbia. During the period from 1957 to 1962 each appellant in these cases purchased a number of household items from Walker-Thomas, for which payment was to be made in installments. The terms of each purchase were contained in a printed form contract which set forth the value of the purchased item and purported to lease the item to appellant for a stipulated monthly rent payment. The contract then provided, in substance, that title would remain in Walker-Thomas until the total of all the monthly payments made equaled the stated value of the item, at which time appellants could take title. In the event of a default in the payment of any monthly installment, Walker-Thomas could repossess the item.

The contract further provided that "the amount of each periodical installment payment to be made by [purchaser] to the Company under this present lease shall be inclusive of and not in addition to the amount of each installment payment to be made by [purchaser] under such prior leases, bills or accounts; and *all payments now and hereafter made by [purchaser] shall be credited pro rata on all outstanding leases, bills and accounts* due the Company by [purchaser] at the time each such payment is made." Emphasis added.) The effect of this

rather obscure provision was to keep a balance due on every item purchased until the balance due on all items, whenever purchased, was liquidated. As a result, the debt incurred at the time of purchase of each item was secured by the right to repossess all the times previously purchased by the same purchaser, and each new item purchased automatically became subject to a security interest arising out of the previous dealings.

On May 12, 1962, appellant Thorne purchased an item described as a Daveno, three tables, and two lamps, having total stated value of $391.10. Shortly thereafter, he defaulted on his monthly payments and appellee sought to replevy all the items purchased since the first transaction in 1958. Similarly, on April 17, 1962, appellant Williams bought a stereo set of stated value of $514.95. She too defaulted shortly thereafter, and appellee sought to replevy all the items purchased since December, 1957. The Court of General Sessions granted judgment for appellee. The District of Columbia Court of Appeals affirmed, and we granted appellants' motion for leave to appeal to this court.

Appellants' principal contention, rejected by both the trial and the appellate courts below, is that these contracts, or at least some of them, are unconscionable and, hence, not enforceable. In its opinion in Williams v. Walker-Thomas Furniture Company, 198 A.2d 914, 916 (1964), the District of Columbia Court of Appeals explained its rejection of this contention as follows:

"Appellant's second argument presents a more serious question. The record reveals that prior to the last purchase appellant had reduced the balance in her account to $164. The last purchase, a stereo set, raised the balance due to $678. Significantly, at the time of this and the preceding purchases, appellee was aware of appellant's financial position. The reverse side of the stereo contract listed the name of appellant's social worker and her $218 monthly stipend from the government. Nevertheless, with full knowledge that appellant had to feed, clothe and support both herself and seven children on this amount, appellee sold her a $514 stereo set.

"We cannot condemn too strongly appellee's conduct. It

raises serious questions of sharp practice and irresponsible business dealings. A review of the legislation in the District of Columbia affecting retail sales and the pertinent decisions of the highest court in this jurisdiction disclose, however, no ground upon which this court can declare the contracts in question contrary to public policy. We note that were the Maryland Retail Installment Sales Act, Art. 83 §§ 128–153, or its equivalent, in force in the District of Columbia, we could grant appellant appropriate relief. We think Congress should consider corrective legislation to protect the public from such exploitive contracts as were utilized in the case at bar."

We do not agree that the court lacked the power to refuse enforcement to contracts found to be unconscionable. In other jurisdictions, it has been held as a matter of common law that unconscionable contracts are not enforceable.

[1, 2] Congress has recently enacted the Uniform Commercial Code, which specifically provides that the court may refuse to enforce a contract which it finds to be unconscionable at the time it was made.

[3–10] Unconscionability has generally been recognized to include an absence of meaningful choice on the part of one of the parties together with contract terms which are unreasonably favorable to the other party. Whether a meaningful choice is present in a particular case can only be determined by consideration of all the circumstances surrounding the transaction. In many cases the meaningfulness of the choice is negated by a gross inequality of bargaining power.

[11–13] In determining reasonableness or fairness, the primary concern must be with the terms of the contract considered in light of the circumstances existing when the contract was made.

[14] Because the trial court and the appellate court did not feel that enforcement could be refused, no findings were made on the possible unconscionability of the contracts in these cases. Since the record is not sufficient for our deciding the issue as a matter of law, the cases must be remanded to the trial court for further proceedings.

So ordered.

Example 3B. Revised opinion

Ora Lee WILLIAMS,
Appellant,

v.

WALKER-THOMAS
FURNITURE
COMPANY, Appellee.

William THORNE
et al., Appellants,

v.

WALKER-THOMAS
FURNITURE
COMPANY, Appellee.

Nos. 18604, 18605

United States Court
of Appeals
District of Columbia Circuit
Argued April 9, 1965.
Decided Aug. 11, 1964.

Background: Appellants signed a series of contracts for furniture. The balance due on every item purchased continued until the total debt for all items was liquidated. The Court of General Sessions found no common law ground by which they could declare the contracts were contrary to public policy and thus found for the furniture company. The District of Columbia Court of Appeals agreed and affirmed that decision.

Holding: This court, however, holds that where a contract is unconscionable due to the term and circumstances of the contract, that contract is unenforceable in a court of law. We therefore reverse the decisions below and remand the cases to the trial court to determine if these circumstances and terms were so unfair and unreasonable that they were unconscionable as a matter of law.

Procedural background and facts of contracts:

J. SKELLY WRIGHT, Circuit Judge:

Appellee, Walker-Thomas Furniture Company, operates a retail furniture store in the District of Columbia. During the period from 1957 to 1962 each appellant in these cases purchased a number of household items from Walker-Thomas, for which payment was to be made in installments. The terms of each purchase were contained in a printed form contract which set forth the value of the purchased item and purported to lease the item to appellant for a stipulated monthly rent payment. The contract then provided, in substance, that title would remain in Walker-Thomas until the total of all the monthly payments made equaled the stated value of the item, at which time appellants could take title. In the event of a default in the payment of any monthly installment, Walker-Thomas could repossess the item.

On May 12, 1962, appellant Thorne purchased an item described as a Daveno, three tables, and two lamps, having total stated value of $391.10. Shortly thereafter, he defaulted on his monthly payments and appellee sought to replevy all the items purchased since the first transaction in 1958. Similarly, on April 17, 1962, appellant Williams bought a stereo set of stated value of $514.95.[1] She too defaulted shortly thereafter, and appellee sought to replevy all the items purchased since December, 1957.

Arguments:

Appellants' principal contention, rejected by both the trial and the appellate courts below, is that these contracts, or at least some of them, are unconscionable and, hence, not enforceable. In its opinion in Williams v. Walker-Thomas Furniture Company, 198 A.2d 914, 916 (1964), the District of Columbia Court of Appeals explained its rejection of this contention as follows:

"Appellant's second argument presents a more serious question. The record reveals that prior to the last purchase appellant had reduced the balance in her account to $164. The last purchase, a stereo set, raised the balance due to $678. Significantly, at the time of this and the preceding purchases, appellee was aware of appellant's financial position. The

reverse side of the stereo contract listed the name of appellant's social worker and her $218 monthly stipend from the government. Nevertheless, with full knowledge that appellant had to feed, clothe and support both herself and seven children on this amount, appellee sold her a $514 stereo set.

Discussion:

A. The Court has the power to refuse enforcement of unconscionable contracts.

We do not agree that the court lacked the power to refuse enforcement to contracts found to be unconscionable. In other jurisdictions, it has been held as a matter of common law that unconscionable contracts are not enforceable.[2] . . .

B. U.C.C. codification of the common law rule of unconscionability is persuasive authority.

[1, 2] Congress has recently enacted the Uniform Commercial Code, which specifically provides that the court may refuse to enforce a contract which it finds to be unconscionable at the time it was made.

1. Circumstances

Whether a meaningful choice is present in a particular case can only be determined by consideration of all the circumstances surrounding the transaction. In many cases the meaningfulness of the choice is negated by a gross inequality of bargaining power.[7] . . .

2. Reasonableness or Fairness

[11–13] In determining reasonableness or fairness, the primary concern must be with the terms of the contract considered in light of the circumstances existing when the contract was made. . . .

Conclusion

[14] Because the trial court and the appellate court did not feel that enforcement could be refused, no findings were made on the possible unconscionability of the contracts in these cases.

EXAMPLE 4A.   Campus sexual harassment policy

SEXUAL HARASSMENT IS AGAINST THE LAW

Definitions

"Sexual harassment"—Title VII of the Civil Rights Act of 1964 (employees), Title IX of the Education Amendments of 1972 (students), and University law define sexual harassment as unwelcome sexual advances; requests for sexual favors and other verbal or physical conduct of a sexual nature when submission to such conduct is made a term or condition of one's academic or employment status or is used as a basis for academic or employment decision; or conduct that unreasonably interferes with one's academic pursuits or working conditions by creating a hostile environment.

"*Quid pro quo* harassment"—When a person with authority in the university uses submission to or rejection of unwelcome sexual conduct as the basis for making academic or employment decisions affecting a subordinate, that action is sexual harassment.

"Harasser"—Sexual harassment can occur between supervisors and subordinates, faculty or staff and students, students' peers or co-workers, contractors or visitors and students, or any combination of these.

"Prohibited conduct"—This includes subtle or overt pressure for sexual activity, unnecessary and unwanted touching or brushing against another's body, stalking, sexually suggestive visual displays and/or obscene messages, deliberate assaults or molestations, demands for sexual favors, or promises of preferential treatment or gifts in exchange for sex.

"Unwelcome behavior"—Behavior will be considered unwelcome if the individual did not solicit or invite it and particularly if he or she indicates that the conduct is undesirable or offensive. Acquiescence or failure to complain does not mean that the conduct is welcome. However, if a student or employee actively participates in sexual banter or discussions without giving an indication that the discussion is offensive, it will not be considered unwelcome.

How to report sexual harassment

Report the incident to the dean of students or the equal opportunity officer. Employees, including students who are employed here, who experience sexual harassment in their workplace, should report it to a supervisor or the equal opportunity officer. All complaints and related documents will be maintained in a confidential file and every attempt will be made to ensure the privacy of the individual and the respondent, subject to the university's legal obligations to take necessary disciplinary steps. If it is determined that sexual harassment has occurred, the university will proceed with disciplinary action with or without agreement from the complainant.

EXAMPLE 4B. Revised sexual harassment policy

SEXUAL HARASSMENT IS AGAINST THE LAW

What is sexual harassment?

Sexual harassment is
◆ unwelcome sexual advances;
◆ requests for sexual favors and other verbal or physical conduct of a sexual nature when submission to that conduct is made a term or condition of one's academic or employment status or is used as a basis for academic or employment decision; or
◆ conduct that unreasonably interferes with one's academic pursuits or working conditions by creating a hostile environment.

What conduct is prohibited?

The law prohibits
◆ subtle or overt pressure for sexual activity,
◆ unnecessary and unwanted touching or brushing against another's body,
◆ stalking, sexually suggestive visual displays and/or obscene messages,
◆ deliberate assaults or molestations,
◆ demands for sexual favors, or
◆ promises of preferential treatment or gifts in exchange for sex.

Example: You are a work-study student and your boss often puts her arm around you or invites you home after work. You refuse those invitations and dread going to work.

Who might be a "harasser"?

Sexual harassment can occur between supervisors and subordinates, faculty or staff and students, students, peers or co-workers, contractors or visitors and students, or any combination of these.

When **a person with authority** in the university uses submission to or rejection of unwelcome sexual conduct as the basis for making academic or employment decisions affecting a subordinate, that action is "quid pro quo" harassment.

Title VII of the Civil Rights Act of 1964 (employees), Title IX of the Education Amendments of 1972 (students), and University law.

How will someone determine "unwelcome" behavior?

Behavior will be considered unwelcome if the individual **did not invite** it and particularly if he or she indicates that the conduct is undesirable or offensive. Failure to complain does not mean that the conduct is welcome.

However, if a student or employee actively participates in sexual banter without indicating that the discussion is offensive, it will not be considered unwelcome.

Example: You are in an office where many of your male co-workers tell jokes about women and sex. You always break away from the group and change the subject.

EXAMPLE 5A. Paragraphs with no variety, unnecessary capitalizations

The State Bar is required to offer CONTINUING LEGAL EDUCATION seminars throughout the state, throughout the year. As part of that mandate, CONTINUING LEGAL EDUCATION courses are offered this month in Alexandria, Annandale, Burke, Centreville, Fairfax, Lorton, Oakton, Reston, Vienna, and Falls Church. The CONTINUING EDUCATION classes will cover topics as diverse as ESTATE PLANNING, FEDERAL CRIMINAL LITIGATION, SECURITIES REGULATIONS, PROFESSIONAL SPORTS AND THE LAW, and FEDERAL AND STATE INDIAN LAW. Each course will be offered for three hours, and repeated twice during the month at each site.

Registration for these courses can be by mail, fax, or e-mail. Registrants must include their bar card number, their date of birth, application fee, and telephone number. Registrants are informed by this notice that they can receive no refund, but the registration fee can be applied to future CONTINUING LEGAL EDUCATION courses. The State Bar must receive the registration form and money five days before the course is presented. An acknowledgement will be sent to the registrant's address, plus a copy will be kept at the entrance to the seminar. Seminars will be conducted by state-certified attorneys with expertise in the field.

EXAMPLE 5B.   Revised paragraph with variety and side bar

CONTINUING LEGAL EDUCATION

The State Bar offers Continuing Legal Education seminars throughout the state, throughout the year. Continuing Legal Education courses are offered this month in

- Alexandria
- Annandale
- Burke
- Centreville
- Fairfax
- Lorton
- Oakton
- Reston
- Vienna
- Falls Church

TOPICS

Estate Planning
Federal Criminal Litigation
Securities Regulations
Professional Sports and the Law
Federal and State Indian Law

Each course will be offered for three hours, and repeated twice during the month at each site.

Registration
Registration for these courses can be by mail, fax, or e-mail. Registrants must include their

bar card number,
date of birth,
application fee, and
telephone number.

Although you can receive no refund, your registration fee can be applied to future CONTINUING LEGAL EDUCATION courses.

The registration form and money must be received five days before the course is presented.

An acknowledgement will be sent to the registrant's address, plus a copy will be kept at the entrance to the seminar. Seminars will be conducted by state-certified attorneys with expertise in the field.

◆ ◆ ◆ ◆

I imagine a writing trauma center: students wheeled in—moaning or even unconscious—with dangling modifiers and split infinitives, their texts soaked in the blood of their last assessment; over here a brave tutor performing an emergency metonymy on otherwise bloodless prose; over there one carefully removing a comma splice from a freshman's summary; a first-year resident looking up from the table in dismay, saying, "I've never seen anything like it. I don't know what to do." And a grizzled veteran taking over: "200 cc's of Strunk 'n White, STAT. and give me Lanham. I'm going to have to cut."
Raul Sanchez, Writing Center, University of Utah

◆ ◆ ◆ ◆

6

REVIEWING THE BASICS

Before leaving law school for law practice, you will want to review those errors the business world considers so egregious that no literate writer would make them. Some so-called rules of grammar are actually not rules but are treated that way by your future employers; depending on your audience, you may or may not adhere to them.[1] Answers are included in the Appendix.

---

[1] For instance, no rule in the English language requires writers to keep infinitives (to run, to write) as integral, unsplit units; nor is there a rule that sentences cannot end in a preposition. Nevertheless, if your boss believes these are rules, then adjust to his or her expectations.

GRAMMAR, PUNCTUATION, WORD CHOICE EXAMINATION 1

1. From the very start, our client has been hostile about Tommie researching his taxes.

2. When looking at the facts of the cases, the holdings were very similar.

3. Mrs. Lovett was discharged in part because of her handicap, however the primary concern of her manager is Mrs. Lovett's inability to perform the functions of her job.

4. Dr. Smith is in a competitive business and requires employees who he can trust to insure the patient's safety and care.

5. If this information proves to be erroneous, the Info'puters would be, and in fact were injured less by revenue than by taxes.

6. The plaintiffs claim that the statements made by the Attorney General's chief representatives is misleading.

7. Bread for the World helped establish a fund for childhood immunizations and other measures to reduce infant mortality abroad. This aided the poorest of the poor.

8. Each of the organizations has their favorite country to help out of poverty.

9. Not concerned with lobbyists in this case is those legislators who have no weapons manufactured in their states.

10. He was arrested for breaking and entering, assault and battery and rape, but he insists that he was in Washington, D.C., during that weekend.

GRAMMAR, PUNCTUATION, WORD CHOICE EXAMINATION 2

1. The congressman sent the letter back to three others and myself who had forgotten to add the documentation.

2. When applying the statute to the case law and the facts provided, it appears that Miss Watson was detained without probable cause.

3. If Mrs. Benjamin is able to prove her prima facie case of employment discrimination the burden then shifts to her employer to set forth a legitimate, nondiscriminatory reason for the dismissal.

4. An alleged tort-feasor would have been at a tactical disadvantage if the lawsuit were delayed by the injured party. This prompted the court to say that it would be in the interest of justice to permit it.

5. The just cause was compelling enough to preclude the defense from providing these "reasonable accommodations." Part of the third element determining the intention of the employer.

6. We did not get to see "Romeo and Juliet," which is a tragedy.

7. Left out overnight, the law professor discovered a missing stack of final exams on his doorstep.

8. The congresswoman could no longer be trusted to vote with her party's line, she no longer had patience with political hair splitters.

9. Mr. Beckman's office is to small to hold the full records tracking legislative votes to relieve third-world debt.

10. It took the team six months just to read through the long, precisely organized contract.

11. A major problem for any student is the application into, education during, and paying loans after law school.

ANSWERS TO "TRY THESE," CONCLUDING EXERCISES, AND REVIEWING THE BASICS

CHAPTER 1: ORGANIZATION

Try These

pp. 10–11 ▶ **1.** Yes, the two headings follow the initial road map, although readers may have assumed that context and form would be discussed separately.

pp. 11–12 ▶ **2.** Yes, the three headings follow the numbered road map.

p. 12 ▶ **3.** The introductory phrase is perhaps a tie-in to a previous point and is also a message to the reader that this next point is not dependent on the one above. The main clause, "The District Court erred . . . ," is a strong, declarative statement. It does not, however, connect to the first sentence of the paragraph. The first sentence is flawed in several ways: it does not tie the specific case to the argument, and it does not function as the topic sentence, which is buried after the elliptical quotation.

Try These

pp. 16–17 ▶ **1.** An employee with a handicap, who can no longer safely perform the job, should be moved to another

job, one the employee can handle safely, if that job is available.

An employer is often limited in ability to accommodate an employee's handicap. "It is not necessary that a new, unneeded position be created but, rather, if a new disability prevents an employee from performing his present job, an effort to place him in an existing position which is vacant and for which he is qualified to perform must be made." [cite] The employer is not required to create positions to accommodate a handicapped employee because that would pose "undue hardship on the conduct of the employer's business." [cite] In <u>Ali v. Chelsea Catering</u>, the court determined that an employer does not fail to accommodate the plaintiff if he does not have any present openings that could be safely filled by the handicapped employee. [cite] ~~The employer is "within its rights to subject the handicapped employee to the full range of disciplinary proceedings up to and including discharge." [cite]~~

An existing safe job for the plaintiff will be the most difficult element of the prima facie case for the plaintiff to establish. Her performance reviews reflect an inability to match professional standards, and she is unable to perform her job safely. ~~The company will suffer financially if she is retained.~~ No other position is available that has a lower level of physical or mental requirements.

Try This

p. 22 ▶ Helen Pergene was employed at the New Orleans South High School as a government teacher and audio visual coordinator from 1995 until September 16, 1999. **Two weeks before she was fired,** on August 30, 1999, Mrs. Pergene appeared on local television as a spokesperson for **"Open Doors,"** a libertarian organization. **Open Doors** lobbies for the legal status of alternative familial **arrangements. The arrangement** Mrs. Peregene discussed during her television **interview** was single-sex adoptions, and she argued for the passage of current legislation. **During her interview,** she revealed an internal school memo from the principal **that** instructed faculty to avoid any mention of the pending legislation.

Concluding Exercises

pp. 22–23 ▶ 1. The paragraph informs readers that there are two rules about learning the identity of people retained for a trial, but who might not expect to actually be witnesses. But the road map sentence lists three aspects of the rules. The reader cannot intuit how the material will be organized: rule by rule? Or will the material begin with textual context (the first aspect) and its relationship to both rules, and then move to the second and third aspect of both rules?

p. 23 ▶ 2. Readers are prepared for #1, General Rule and Specificity. #2, Case Law is ineffective as a heading. Because the road map attaches its "several Second Circuit cases have discussed and applied" language to the sentence introducing civil rights as a subset, readers probably are looking for the civil rights language. #3, Counteranalysis, is totally different language from "considerations" that "weigh against." None of the headings applies the legal points to the case.

pp. 23–24 ▶ 3. **If an act of thievery is witnessed by an employee, courts have held that store personnel have probable cause to detain and question the customer.** In <u>Freeman</u>, the court ruled that there was reasonable suspicion because both the store clerk and the store manager witnessed the customer's putting her hand down her shirt while standing at the earring display rack. <u>Freeman v. Kar Way Inc.</u>, 686 So.2d 53 (La. Ct.

App. 1998). **Similarly,** in <u>Derouen</u>, an employee witnesses the customer placing a bag of shrimp in her shopping bag and then placing an object in her purse. <u>Derouen v. Miller</u>, 614 So.2d 1306 (La. Ct. App. 1993). In Miss Miller's case, the issue presented is whether the store manager had probable cause to detain Miss Miller under the context of the code.

p. 24 ▶ **4.** The store clerk turned to assist a customer. **A short time later,** the clerk saw that both Miss Dobrowski and the necklace were gone, **so she** immediately called a manager. The manager saw Miss Dobrowski, who matched the description the clerk gave, and quickly got her attention. He **immediately** informed Miss Dobrowski that she was a suspect. Miss Dobrowski denied that she had taken anything from the store and refused to go with the manager for questioning. **After the refusal,** the manager grabbed Miss Dobrowski and detained her in the office. Miss Dobrowski protested loudly as the manager took her through the store. **Nevertheless,** the manager physically placed her in the office, locked the door, **and left** to take care of another incident. **After completing that task, the manager** went to find the clerk who had reported the theft. Half an **hour after he had left Miss Dobrowski,** he returned with the clerk, who could not positively identify Miss Dobrowski. **At that point,** the manager asked Miss Dobrowski to empty her purse, **and** she complied. The manager found no jewelry, **so** he allowed Miss Dobrowski to leave the store.

p. 24 ▶ **5.** In the first paragraph, briefly introduce the two rules: intent in causing harm to an unintended recipient of the harm and actual harm differing from intended harm. Then create a paragraph on each, using the cases. Next, show the similarities between the Lima case and the precedent. In another paragraph, present the counterargument with a topic sentence about the double transfer. It should be followed with the response to that counterargument. The last paragraph needs a topic sentence announcing its policy argument.

CHAPTER 2: SENTENCES

Try These

p. 31 ▶ **1.** A Cuban journalist has been jailed for four years, **said** dissident sources and the international press freedom-watchdog group, Reporters Without Borders.

p. 31 ▶ **2.** <u>Klopps v. Adonis</u> **involves a tangible form of property.** <u>Klopps</u> is unlike the kind of in rem action typified by <u>Harris v. Balk</u>, 198 U.S. 215 (1905), in which the property attached was an intangible debt owed by one person to another.

p. 31 ▶ **3.** With proper rules, if their members and registered animals are regularly involved in unregistered meets or illegal activities related to racing, the nonstatutory breed registries (Appaloosa, Arabian, etc.) could **(1)** lose their registry status **or (2)** have their animals barred from pari-mutuel competitions.

p. 31 ▶ **4.** **Due immediately in the event of a default on a payment is** the entire amount of an employer's withdrawal liability plus accrued interest on the total outstanding liability from the due date of the first payment that was not timely made. 29 U.S.C. § 1399(c)(5).

Try These

p. 33 ▶ **1.** **A juror may** be more sympathetic if the juror and the defendant are of the same socioeconomic class, or if the juror is in a higher class than the defendant, ~~depending on the voir dire and the nature of the case.~~ **The juror may even** be disposed to give the defendant a break.

p. 33 ▶ **2.** **The Commission accepted** the District's application after its general counsel noted that the District would have the opportunity to contest the necessity for the proposed halfway house. **The District's opportunity will come** at the upcoming hearing on its application for an amendment to its halfway housing permits.

Try These

p. 35 ▶ **1.** **The four standards** of "negligent misrepresentation" are set forth in <u>Atkins v. Kirkpatrick</u>, 832 S.W.2d 547 (Tenn. Ct. App. 1991).

p. 35 ▶ **2.** **The Louisiana Criminal Code** governs this case. La. Code Crim. Proc. Ann. Art 215 (West 1987).

p. 35 ▶ **3.** Even a single wheat farmer's decision to plant his own crop was held to fall under the third category of interstate commerce regulation, <u>Wickard v. Filburn</u>, 317 U.S. 111 (1942). **Thus,** Congress was empowered to regulate his activity.

p. 35 ▶ **4.** **Section 1399** allows the employer to seek review of the schedule of payments. 29 U.S.C. Section 1399(b)(2)(A)(i). However, this dispute also falls under Section 1401, the arbitration provision.

Try These

p. 39 ▶ **1.** Christi Mayhem tried "at least 10 times" to leave Cornelius Fenwick, father of her two baby boys. She said **Fenwick would beat** her regularly.

p. 39 ▶ **2.** Article 2.11(B) requires diligence to be used to locate the registered agent **only** at the registered address.

p. 39 ▶ **3.** He claims the psychiatrist contradicted himself during the competency hearing, **however,** by stating affirmatively that Porter was competent to stand trial. *Or* **However, he** claims . . .

Try These

p. 42 ▶ **1.** It is the type of bureaucratic abuse that, unless someone complains about it, ~~that~~ is going to continue.

p. 43 ▶ **2.** The plaintiff must show:
(1) a reasonable probability that the parties would enter into a contractual relationship;
(2) **the** defendant acted maliciously by intentionally
preventing the relationship from occurring with
the purpose of harming the plaintiff;
(3) the defendant was not privileged or justified; and
(4) actual harm or damage occurred as a result of the
interference.

p. 43 ▶ **3.** Training first-year instructors plus advertising and interviewing **them** [*or* **first-year** instructors] is a major
institutional expense.

Try These

p. 46 ▶ **1.** To constitute fraud or **to be** a ground of rescission,
there must **be not only** a representation as to an existing fact **but that** representation must have been false;
it must have been relied on, and it must have been so
material that it determined the conduct of the party
seeking relief.

p. 46 ▶ **2.** If a Louisiana store manager detains the customer
without probable cause, detains the customer for over
an hour, or uses unnecessary bodily force causing injury, **then** a customer has a cause of action for false
imprisonment. [*or*, A customer has . . . if . . .]

p. 46 ▶ **3.** **A merchant must end** the detention as soon as possible ~~if detention is warranted~~ if there is no additional
reasonable cause.

121

Try These

p. 48 ▶ **1.** The secretary **misplaced** the file.

p. 48 ▶ **2.** **This court recently considered** the right to trial by jury in administrative license revocation proceedings in <u>Adams v. Texas State Board of Chiropractic Examiners</u>, 744 S.W.2d 648 (Tex. App.—Austin 1988, no writ).

p. 48 ▶ **3.** **The hearing established that** Mrs. Brown was currently on deferred adjudication probation for theft over $200.00. **This hearing was** outside the presence of a jury on the defendant's motion to suppress the identification testimony.

p. 48 ▶ **4.** The loan was approved by the Lincoln Bank Board of Directors and was on file as an official record of the depository institution. [**Leave first verb passive**—the emphasis is, correctly, on the loan. Plus, the loan is the subject of the second verb phrase and is therefore in the correct position.]

p. 49 ▶ **5.** The United States Supreme Court **broadened** this theme in <u>Tully v. Griffin, Inc.</u>, **holding** that a federal court is "under an equitable duty" to not interfere with a state's collection of its revenue except when "an asserted federal right might otherwise be lost." [**Strengthen with active.**]

Try These

p. 52 ▶ **1.** The Supreme Court delineated between unreasonable contracts that are void or not void for fraud: "If a contract be unreasonable and unconscionable, but not void for fraud, a court of law will give to the party who sues for its breach damages, not according to its letter, but only such as he is equitably entitled to." <u>In Scott v. United States</u>, 79 U.S. (12 Wall.) 443, 445, 20 L.Ed. 438 (1970). Since we have never adopted or rejected such a rule, the question here is actually one of first impression.

p. 52 ▶ 2. Under Florida law, prejudgment interest is proper in a specific performance decree. Defendants rely on a **1978 district court case** to claim that when damages are not liquidated until time of judgment, the claim is one for unliquidated damages and prejudgment interest must be denied. <u>Town of Longboat Key v. Carl E. Widell & Son</u>, 362 So.2d 719 (Fla. Dist. Ct. App. 1978). **However,** the Florida Supreme Court has discredited the test espoused in <u>Town of Longboat</u> by adopting the test that a claim becomes liquidated and susceptible of prejudgment interest <u>where the trial court's order fixes the amounts due as of specific dates</u>. <u>Hurley v. Slingerland</u>, 480 So.2d 104, 107 (Fla. Dist. Ct. App. 1985), citing <u>Argonaut Ins. Co. v. May Plumbing Co.</u>, 474 So.2d 212 (Fla. 1985).

p. 52 ▶ 3. **Alaska statute** defines marriages as a "civil contract entered into by one man and one woman that requires both a license and a solemnization." A.S. 25.05.011

Concluding Exercises

Sentence Quiz 1:

citation ▶ 1. Defendant G & E may be entitled to qualified
placement, immunity from a **Section 1983** civil action. 28
passive U.S.C. § 1983; therefore, the **court must determine** whether defendant G & E's conduct violated any clearly established statutory or constitutional right.

if/then ▶ 2. **If** the district court has failed to provide reasons for its decision to deny an indigent civil litigant's request for counsel, **then** the court of appeals in some cases may have to remand **because**, without the district court's reasons, the appellate court may not be able to determine whether the district court made a reasoned and informed decision regarding the appointment of counsel.

separation ▶ 3. This **Court stated** in the earlier order that it had
subject and received the Defendant's Reply, which contained
verb the first fraud-on-the-court argument. **That**
statement is certainly some indication that it was
considered.

citations ▶ 4. Quasi-in-rem jurisdiction was first based on the
as subjects conceptual basis of state sovereignty. **An 1878**
United States Supreme Court case held that a
state has sovereign power over property and persons within its borders, and over nothing outside
of them. Pennoyer v. Neff, 95 U.S. 714 (1878).
Thus a state could legitimately require a nonresident to come into the state to defend a cause of
action, or forfeit his forum property. **Almost a**
hundred years later, the same court, in Shaffer
v. Heitner, 433 U.S. 186 (1977), held that all assertions of state court power must meet standards of due process as articulated in another
Supreme Court case, International Shoe v. Washington, 326 U.S. 310 (1945).

placement ▶ 5. Female applicants were asked about plans for future children. Male applicants, **however,** were
not. [*or* However, male . . .]

parallelism ▶ 6. Other provisions of Section 6 provide **for** the
requisites of the application for a bondsman's li-
cense, **for** an investigation and hearing by the
board, and **for** its denial of the application or approval conditioned on the applicant's filing of the
required security deposits.

front-loaded ▶ 7. Parents frustrate their children and make them
sentence feel helpless **by** losing sight of the "delicate interweaving of the child's developmental tasks with
the entangled web of parental conflict" **and by**
imposing changes in custody and access arrangements on ill-equipped children.

parallelism ▶ 8. The court can force a child to visit the noncustodial parent only after the judge has (1) **afforded**

parties a hearing, (2) **created** proper court order based on findings of fact and conclusions of law, and (3) **made** findings that include incarceration of a parent if it is reasonably necessary for the welfare of the child.

incorporating ▶ 9. This obligation is not dependent upon Border's
quotations intention to submit to arbitration, but rather is imposed on the "[c]orporation under the [statute]." ILGWU Nat'l Retirement Fund v. Levy Bros. Frocks, 846 F.2d 859, 885 (2d Cir. 1988).

incorporating ▶ 10. Our client was caught during a robbery. She is
quotations not guilty of kidnapping:
over 50
words
> Kidnapping is the unlawful movement by physical force of a person against his will and without his consent for a substantial distance where such movement is not merely incidental to the commission of the robbery and where such movement substantially increases the risk of significant physical injuries to such person over and above those in which such person is normally exposed in the commission of the crime of robbery itself.

Roland v. Borg, No. 93-56111, 1994 WL 383840 (9th Cir. 1994).

Sentence Quiz 2:

ambiguous ▶ 1. A 1977 court found the custodial mother in con-
reference tempt despite the children's claims that they refused to visit with their father because he abused them. **The court** thus declared that the ultimate responsibility rests with the custodial parent who cannot escape his/her duty to comply with the provisions of the decree by attempting to shift the burden to the discretion of her children.

citation ▶ 2. The general rule is that an attorney cannot be
placement held liable to third parties for acts committed
within the scope of attorney-client relationship,
absent fraud or negligence in the drafting of
an estate planning document. <u>Anderson v.
McBurney</u>, 467 N.W.2d 158, 160 (Wis. Ct. App.
1991); <u>Brown v. LaChance</u>, 477 N.W.2d 296, 300
(Wis. Ct. App. 1991). This exception has been
narrowly construed by the courts of Wisconsin,
which have held it valid in a limited context.

placement ▶ 3. Agent further acknowledges that Owner will accept financing of the sale through **only one** of
the four following methods.

parallelism ▶ 4. The plaintiff **was not hindered** in the prosecution of his case because he was confined, **nor forbidden** access to legal documents.

parallelism ▶ 5. It was thus impossible to determine **if** the conduct was protected by the first amendment, and
under the <u>Nearich</u> test **if** the allegations were insufficient.

front- ▶ 6. Although the court was required to assess the ev-
loaded and idence presented in light most favorable to the
ambiguous, plaintiff, Aziz, **he nevertheless failed** to establish
citation the "serious" nature of his injury through expert
witness. The **plaintiff could not prove that the
facts established** the "deliberate indifference"
standard required in Section 1983. 42 U.S.C. Section 1983.

parallelism ▶ 7. The main reason ~~that~~ the strikers did not cross
the picket lines was that they wanted to show
solidarity to the management.

citation ▶ 8. Case law reasons that a jury informed of the pos-
placement sibility of commuting a life sentence might conclude that an error of judgment on its part would
be corrected by another body of government.
See Kimberly Metzer, "Resolving the 'False
Dilemma': Simmons v. South Carolina and the

Capital Sentencing Jury's Access to Parole Ineligibility Information," 27 U. Tol. Rev. 149, 167-173 (1995).

citation ▶ 9. Paraguay **is not** within a United States jurisdiction, **nor** a "person" in Section 1983. *See* <u>Moor v. County of Alameda</u>, 411 U.S. 693, 699 (1973); <u>South Carolina v. Katzenbach</u>, 383 U.S. 301, 323-24 (1966).

placement

long ▶ 10. If the list that follows the colon makes up an integral part of the introductory sentence, writers should remember

sentence; tabulate

(a) to indent all of each item and to number each item;

(b) to begin each item with a lower-case letter;

(c) to end each item except the last with a semi-colon;

(d) to use a semicolon and "and" or "or" on the next-to-last item; and

(e) to conclude the last item with a period unless the list does not conclude the sentence.

CHAPTER 3: WORDS

Try These

p. 61 ▶ 1. TO THE HONORABLE JUDGE ~~OF SAID COURT.~~

~~NOW COME~~ defendants ~~in the above styled and numbered cause and file this their~~ Motion for Directed Verdict~~, and~~ request[s] that the court direct the jury to return a verdict ~~in this cause~~ and ~~in support~~ would show ~~as follows~~: . . .

p. 61 ▶ 2. The prisoner was a better *pro se* litigant than many of the uneducated plaintiffs before the court.

p. 61 ▶ 3. Don Miller refutes this charge and contends that he has been unfairly brought into this suit as a party.

127

p. 61 ▶ 4. She alleges violation of certain state law claims: fraud, breach of contract, and misrepresentation.

Try These

p. 65 ▶ 1. to evaluate

p. 65 ▶ 2. destroyed

p. 65 ▶ 3. said

p. 65 ▶ 4. agreement

p. 65 ▶ 5. The teacher was morally, but not legally, obligated.

p. 65 ▶ 6. At a hearing requesting a temporary injunction, the only question is whether the applicant is entitled to preserve status quo of the subject matter until a final trial.

Try These

p. 67 ▶ 1. The question is whether Smith informed others of the defect in the computer board design and **if this revealed information** caused the loss of benefits Dell expected from these companies.

p. 67 ▶ 2. If there are cases on point with similar fact situations and you are discussing an issue that calls for argument, **these similar facts** will give more weight to your argument.

p. 67 ▶ 3. Thus, the "IV-D" plan requires that the State pursue reimbursement from absent parents for the public assistance provided for the necessary support of their children. The distribution of collections adheres to **that requirement.**

Try These

p. 69 ▶ 1. certified, return-receipt-amounts postcard receipt *or* certified-return receipt-amounts postcard receipt

p. 69 ▶ 2. funded welfare-insurance programs *or* funded-welfare insurance programs

p. 69 ▶ 3. the bank's contract credit-review service

Try These

p. 71 ▶ 1. After ~~thorough~~ **investigating** of your deposition files, we advise ~~that~~ new coding ~~is a necessary future addition~~.

p. 71 ▶ 2. Thank you for allowing our firm to ~~make our~~ present~~ation of~~ international issues related to your business.

p. 71 ▶ 3. The consultant arrangement makes the transfer of testimony legitimate.

Try These

p. 73 ▶ 1. Nothing in this case warrants applying for a different standard **from** that in <u>Estelle v. Gamble</u>.

p. 73 ▶ 2. **When** the clerk turned back to face his customer, he noticed the necklace and customer were gone.

p. 73 ▶ 3. Dr. Jones suggested that Mrs. Baker hire someone to monitor her work and **ensure** that medicine was properly charted.

p. 73 ▶ 4. The therapist posited various possible cases for the child's anxiety, **e.g.,** travel between two households, parental inability to communicate, incorporation into contrasting religious activities, and concern for both parents, etc.

Try These

p. 75 ▶ 1. Dear J.W. Smith *or* Dear Banker

p. 75 ▶ 2. Use plural: . . . artists need insurance when they . . .

p. 75 ▶ 3. If time and logic permit, exchange the "he" with "she." If the entire document is on its way out the door, attach a note asking if she would want you to ignore tradition and exchange the pronouns in future work you'll do for her.

Concluding Exercises

Word Quiz 1:

pronoun ▶
antecedent

1. It is well established that the design of roads and bridges is a discretionary function, and the State will not be liable for such decisions. **This lack of liability** is consistent with cases that hold decisions made at the policy level instead of operational level are immune.

wordiness ▶

2. Because few attended, we do not know the status of work items and cannot meet the schedule.

nominalizations ▶
wordiness

3. Thank you for helping resolve these issues.

noun strings ▶

4. Parent-company debt-service requirements

pronoun ▶
antecedent

5. Each member of the law school community must report to the Associate Dean any conduct he or she has reason to believe violated the Rules of Professional Conduct; this conduct should raise a question as to the honesty, trustworthiness, or fitness of the student to become a lawyer.

wordiness ▶

6. Please organize the current files concerning the deposition of V. Miles.

noun string ▶

7. six-inch thick concrete pallets *or* six inch-thick concrete pallets

Correct! ▶

8. The sales price would have been taxable whether or not the book was sold directly to the vendors or to the end consumer. (necessary "or not")

gender-based ▶
language

9. When a pilot arrives in the cockpit, he or she needs to review all current logs and check his or her gauges before take-off. *Or make the noun plural:* When pilots arrive . . . they . . . their

treacherous ▶
words

10. The labor law course has as its goal the delineation of workers and bosses.

Word Quiz 2:

wordiness ▶ **1.** The statute's definition must be applied to prove that a person is guilty.

pronoun ▶ **2.** The municipality would have the information
antecedent, concerning the location of the arrest and the
gender-based identity of the co-defendant **police officer** in its
language possession, and the defendant could easily combine this information with the information contained in the complaint. The **municipality's information** will probably provide a sufficiently specific factual basis for the time of the alleged violation, the place where it occurred, and those responsible.

noun string ▶ **3.** well-established common-law cause of action

wordy ▶ **4.** This effort was made callously.

noun string ▶ **5.** the correct substantive-evidence rule test

nominalization ▶ **6.** The Commission's revised rules comprehensively addressed the question of beneficial ownership.

wordy ▶ **7.** ~~It is important to note that~~ the earlier discussion of ~~the~~ computing time periods is relevant here. . . . However, ~~it must be noted that~~ under one statutory interpretation, the ninety-day period is computed from the original due date.

pronoun ▶ **8.** The court in <u>Matthews</u> held that where "plain,
antecedents adequate, and complete" relief is available, the aggrieved party "is left to that remedy in the state courts" unless a federal question is involved. 284 U.S. 526 (1927). Following the enactment of Section 1341 in 1937, **this state-remedy theme** was broadened by the United States Supreme Court.

treacherous ▶ **9.** It **cannot** be said that the plaintiff created a pas-
words sive web site.

gender-based ▶ **10.** When medical **experts** gives evidence through-
language out the trial, **they** must weigh the seriousness of the injury against both **their** medical expertise and professional experiences.

CHAPTER 4: PUNCTUATION

Concluding Exercises

Punctuation Quiz 1:

introductory phrase ▶ **1.** However, to be granted judicial relief for misappropriation of a trade **secret,** the plaintiff must prove by a preponderance of the evidence the following elements.

semicolons for lists with internal commas ▶ **2.** The suit should have been brought against M.B. Beazly, Administrator of the **estate;** Mike Koby, the attorney for the **estate;** and Jim Mattox, the Attorney General.

two independent clauses with "and" ▶ **3.** The issue of the insolvency of a debtor is a question of **fact,** and solvency may be determined proximately before or immediately after the time of the transfer.

run-on ▶ **4.** Not many graduates are without major **debts;** certainly we can list none from our section. (or dash)

colon before lists ▶ **5.** The common law doctrine of negligence consists of three essential **elements:** a legal duty owed by one person to another, a breach of that duty, and damages proximately caused by that breach.

unnecessary colon before short quotation; no beginning ellipses ▶ **6.** Course and scope of employment is defined in Section 101.001(B)(4) as "the performance for a governmental unit of the duties of an employee's office of employment and includes being in or about the performance of tasks lawfully assigned to an employee by competent authority."

essential/ nonessential phrases ▶ **7.** The attorney returned her **fee, which** was under dispute. Or "fee that was" meaning more than one fee

quotation marks with commas; series ▶ **8.** Mr. Marshall also claims that during the arrest Officer Breeger became "highly **abusive,"** denied Mr. Marshall his right to **speak, and** struck the plaintiff twice, without provocation, causing him bodily injury.

dash to set off explanatory information ▶ **9.** In the decision in <u>Santex</u>, supra, the court also held that the employee need prove only that filing the claim was a reason for **termination—not** the sole reason.

fragment ▶ **10.** Plaintiff further argued that the statute did not apply because the unit was only a component part of a larger **whole,** thus not, by itself, an "improvement."

Punctuation Quiz 2

interrupting phrase ▶ **1.** Such participation, he **claims,** was fundamentally unfair.

no punctuation before adverb following verb ▶ **2.** The audit was **correct because** the seven customer contracts stated material and equipment, labor, and sales tax as separated amounts.

series ▶ **3.** The second issue of first impression is whether the reservation of the power to prosecute, compromise and **settle, or** otherwise deal with any claim for additional royalties is illegal and voids any attempt to engage in the unauthorized practice of law.

run-on phrase defines or limits previous phrase ▶ **4.** Each of the Constitution's Amendments has the same **purpose:** each protects us from ourselves. (or dash)

fragment ▶ **5.** A statement apparently made to the EEOC by Weeks shows that Weeks spends only 50% of his time developing new **business, whereas** Johnson spent all of his time developing new business.

citation punctuation ▶ **6.** This Court, in <u>Benson v. McMahon</u>, 127 U.S. 457, 463 **(1888),** has equated this showing to that required for a preliminary hearing in domestic arrest situations.

hyphen/dash; neither requires space around it ▶ **7.** The defendant hoped to ignore the notice—pretend she did not receive it.

no ▶
apostrophe
for plural

8. The company sent twelve **1040s** on the same day.

no ellipses to ▶
begin a
quotation;
ellipses
require
spaces

9. <u>In re Extradition of Russell</u>, the Court of Appeals for the Fifth Circuit echoed the Second Circuit's reasoning:

> the 'information' was allowed to be informal in character, as opposed to substance . . . the provisional arrest request . . . could be made directly between the Justice ministries . . .

short ▶
introductory
phrase needs
comma if
confusing

10. In the first **class,** students were called on alphabetically.

CHAPTER 6: BASICS

Grammar, Punctuation, Word Choice Examination 1

gerund ▶
(possessive)
before pronoun

1. From the very start, our client has been hostile about **Tommie's** researching his taxes.

dangling (-ing ▶
verb modifies
closest noun)

2. When looking at the facts of the cases, the **new attorneys** holdings were very similar.

comma splice ▶
needs period or
semicolon

3. Mrs. Lovett was discharged in part because of her **handicap; however,** the primary concern of her manager is Mrs. Lovett's inability to perform the functions of her job.

direct object ▶
"whom" and
"ensure" (to
make certain,
safe)

4. Dr. Smith is in a competitive business and requires employees **whom** he can trust to **ensure** the patient's safety and care. (he can trust whom)

punctuate ▶
both sides of
interruptor

5. If this information proves to be erroneous, the Info'puters would be, and in fact **were,** injured less by revenue than by taxes.

subject ▶
(statements)/
verb
agreement

6. The plaintiffs claim that the statements made by the Attorney General's chief representatives **are** misleading.

ambiguous ▶ 7. Bread for the World helped establish a fund for
pronoun childhood immunizations and other measures to
reduce infant mortality abroad. **This money**
aided the poorest of the poor.

pronoun ▶ 8. Each of the organizations has **its** favorite country
agreement to help out of poverty. (*or*: The organizations
have their favorite countries . . .)

subject ▶ 9. Not concerned with lobbyists in this case **are**
(legislators)/ those legislators who have no weapons manufac-
verb tured in their states.
agreement

punctuation ▶ 10. He was arrested for breaking and entering, as-
of series sault and **battery,** and rape, but he insists that he
was in Washington, D.C., during that weekend.

Grammar, Punctuation, Word Choice Examination 2

objective, ▶ 1. The congressman sent the letter back to the three
not reflective, others and **me** who had forgotten to add the doc-
pronoun umentation. (*or* back to me and the three others)

dangling ▶ 2. When applying the statute to the case law and
(-ing) verb the facts provided, **the public defender insisted**
modifies that Miss Watson was detained without probable
closest noun cause.

introductory ▶ 3. If Mrs. Benjamin is able to prove her prima facie
clause requires case of employment **discrimination,** the burden
comma then shifts to her employer to set forth a legitimate, nondiscriminatory reason for the dismissal.

ambiguous ▶ 4. An alleged tort-feasor would have been at a tac-
pronouns tical disadvantage if the lawsuit were delayed by
"this" and "it" the injured party. This **possible delay** prompted
the court to say that it would be in the interest of
justice to permit **a timely trial**.

fragment ▶ 5. The just cause was compelling enough to preclude the defense from providing these "reasonable **accommodations," part** of the third element
determining the intention of the employer.

ambiguous ▶ **6.** We did not get to see "Romeo and Juliet," a
pronoun
"which" tragedy. (*or* . . . Romeo and Juliet," which made
the evening a tragedy for us.)

misplaced ▶ **7.** The law professor discovered a missing stack of
phrase final exams, left out overnight on his doorstep.

comma splice ▶ **8.** The congresswoman could no longer be trusted
requires
period or to vote with her party's **line; she** no longer had
semicolon patience with political hair splitters.

to/too/two ▶ **9.** Mr. Beckman's office is **too** small to hold the full
records tracking legislative votes to relieve third-
world debt.

CORRECT. First ▶ **10.** It took the team six months just to read through
adjective
(long) the long, precisely organized contract.
modifies
"contract"
and needs
comma
separation;
"precisely"
already has -ly
as adverb and
can't use
hyphen

parallelism ▶ **11.** A major problem for any student is the application into, education during, and **payment** of
loans after law school.

INDEX